PEACE OF
God

PEACE OF

God

Finding and preserving that precious factor in our lives.

—*Jim Rannells*

JIM RANNELLS

Library of Congress Control Number: 2019910496

PAPERBACK: 978-1-7334028-9-7
EBOOK: 978-1-7334396-0-2

Ordering Information:

For orders and inquiries, please contact:
1-888-404-1388
www.goldtouchpress.com
book.orders@goldtouchpress.com

Printed in the United States of America

THE LEGEND OF THE PRAYING HANDS PAINTING

Back in the fifteenth century, in a tiny village near Nuremberg, lived a family with eighteen children. Eighteen!

In order merely to keep food on the table for this mob, the father and head of the household, a goldsmith by profession, worked almost eighteen hours a day at his trade and any other paying chore he could find in the neighborhood.

Despite their seemingly hopeless condition, two of the elder children, Albrecht and Albert, had a dream. They both wanted to pursue their talent for art, but they knew full well that their father would never be financially able to send either of them to Nuremberg to study at the Academy.

After many long discussions at night in their crowded bed, the two boys finally worked out a pact. They would toss a coin. The loser would go down into the nearby mines and, with his earnings, support his brother while he attended the academy. Then, when that brother who won the toss completed his studies, in four years, he would support the other brother at the academy, either with sales of his artwork or, if necessary, also by laboring in the mines.

They tossed a coin on a Sunday morning after church. Albrecht Durer won the toss and went off to Nuremberg.

Albert went down into the dangerous mines and, for the next four years, financed his brother, whose work at the academy was almost an immediate sensation. Albrecht's etchings, his woodcuts, and his oils were far better than those of most of his professors, and by the time he graduated, he was beginning to earn considerable fees for his commissioned works.

When the young artist returned to his village, the Durer family held a festive dinner on their lawn to celebrate Albrecht's triumphant homecoming. After a long and memorable meal, punctuated with music and laughter, Albrecht rose from his honored position at the head of the table to drink a toast to his beloved brother for the years of sacrifice that had enabled Albrecht to fulfill his ambition. His closing words were, "And now, Albert, blessed brother of mine, now it is your turn. Now you can go to Nuremberg to pursue your dream, and I will take care of you."

All heads turned in eager expectation to the far end of the table where Albert sat, tears streaming down his pale face, shaking his lowered head from side to side while he sobbed and repeated, over and over, "No... No... No... No."

Finally, Albert rose and wiped the tears from his cheeks. He glanced down the long table at the faces he loved, and then, holding his hands close to his right cheek, he said softly, "No, brother. I cannot go to Nuremberg. It is too late for me. Look... Look what four years in the mines have done to my hands! The bones in every finger have been smashed at least once, and lately I have been suffering from arthritis so badly in my right hand that I cannot even hold a glass to return your toast, much less make delicate lines on parchment or canvas with a pen or a brush. No, brother... for me it is too late."

More than 450 years have passed. By now, Albrecht Durer's hundreds of masterful portraits, pen and silver-point sketches, water colors, charcoals, woodcuts, and copper engravings hang in every great museum in the world, but the odds are great that you, like most people, are familiar with only one of Albrecht Durer's works. More than merely being familiar with it, you very well may have a reproduction hanging in your home or office.

One day, to pay homage to Albert for all that he had sacrificed, Albrecht Durer painstakingly drew his brother's abused hands with palms together and thin fingers stretched skyward. He called his powerful drawing simply "Hands," but the entire world almost immediately opened their hearts to his great masterpiece and renamed his tribute of love "The Praying Hands." The next time you see a copy of that touching creation, take a second look. Let it be your reminder, that no one - no one - ever makes it alone!

From: truthbook.com

I want to add that "no one ever makes it alone, because it is the added Grace of God that works in you to develop the talents that He has given an individual."

In my life I have realized that I have been Blessed with several talents and interests----Singing, Painting and more recently, Writing. I try to give God the Glory or try to express His Glory in each of my pursuits---or I am always striving to learn to do such more.

I endeavored to express my version of the painting Albrecht Durer expressed some 450 years before on the cover of this book --- with my interpretation of his painting or a picture of my painting. And, to express that praying to God is the very first step in Seeking Peace, as well as a continued need for that aspect

ACKNOWLEDGMENTS

First and certainly foremost, I want to acknowledge Christ Who has been with me every step of the way in my life, even the times when I was an unbeliever, as I have realized since. He is the Finisher of my Faith [Hebrews 12:2]; and those I have listed here have planted many seeds in my life.

I want to thank the members of the Worland Methodist Church, the pastor, and the members of the Basin Methodist Church. It was them who at the very first, brought out a partial Faith in my deceased wife that eventually developed further in me and through my life.

To Carrol Brown who established in me a feeling of need to use my talent of singing; I sang in his choir for about twenty years.

To Mary Evelyn Bower for the encouragement she provided in the love of music that has developed in me for fifty-some years; I am now singing in another choir with her and have been able to thank her personally for what she instilled in me.

My sister Lori and her husband Ken, who through the years have provided me so much encouragement as they live Blessedly close by; to their daughter Teri, who's such a wonderful example of living in faith as she has been in a wheelchair for some twenty-two years.

To my parents [who are now deceased], for the many wonderful aspects and strengths to my life in which I can now build upon; my mother who essentially taught me to examine things, not unlike what is said in the verse of I Thess. 5:21---"test all things, hold fast to what is good". I solidly believe I will meet her in heaven along with my dad.

My two other sisters, I wish to acknowledge, particularly, Debi and her husband "Whiz" who provided me with much encouragement through the years, despite our differences in our Faiths.

My daughter, Dawn who through the years has loved me back as her imperfect, perfect father; she and her husband Cory did a lot of editing on this book. I am going to sing that song to you, Dawn, [Butterfly Kisses] someday, as it is the perfect tribute to you as my daughter, who has been with me through thick and thin as you were growing up.

My oldest daughter, Amber, who I still pray that God will allow a perfect relationship with us; I pray for her loss of Addison and do not exactly know how to truly share her pain (yet). I thank God that our relationship has already started healing as I and my family spent Christmas Day with her and her family on December 2018.

I wish to thank Barbara Greene, who brought out that love of music in me as I used to sing with her as she played the piano, sharing music at the Nursing Homes. I do try to carry on that tradition of sharing now, in my retirement.

To Kent Dempsey who was the patient pastor/shepherd of the 1st Baptist Church here in Basin and his wife Jan, who also showed her examples on how to worship the Lord in a song. You two were there at the right time in my life and to many other members of this Church, who also encouraged me through the years.

To Phil and Berta Mills, who have given much encouragement for my first book; this one as well and for the encouragement, they both gave me before coming to a True Faith.

To Kay Mowry, who looked out for my two children [Larry and Dawn] after their mother's death; they were 10 and 11 years old when their mother died. She urged them to attend services at a Christian Church, most especially that both were Saved back in 1994 at the Church's Summer Camp; it was a remembrance of that fact that I now assured I will meet my son in heaven and certainly Dawn as she recently returned to the "fold" of Believers.

To Pastor Mike McMillan, who was just the right pastor at the right time to officiate at my son's funeral in 1995. He added so much to my growth in Christ. He planted many seeds in me as I was going through the process of denying my former Mormon Faith.

And to my wife Marti, who has encouraged me through the years in my endeavor to write books and share my Faith. As we are learning more as to "two becomes one", when I realize she is down, somewhat distant from God, I usually find that I am also the same. And, of course, my four other children [Mat, Rachel, Casey, and Jasper] who God told me to love; I am now experiencing the rewards of the Love that I have tried to give them.

CONTENTS

MAKING THE CASE FOR PEACE

"We can have happiness without peace, but then peace would and really should--- include happiness."

---Author quotation

I am not sure if I got that basic notion from a Christian author at one time, but it makes perfect sense to me, as there is a vast difference between the two.

As a very profound example, you would certainly not be in any way happy after you found your only son died from suicide. But, shortly after that moment in my life, I found the start of peace. Since my son's death, It has been a 24-year learning experience to learn from Christ all that peace entails and how to gain it and preserve it.

Happiness is fleeting ---as a moment in time, you can be happy because things are going perfect, and then an hour later you can be filled with sadness that takes away these feelings of happiness. Happiness can come and go--- even many times a day and it is very dependent on how well your life is going at any given moment. It is a fleshly feeling that can change with the wind. We can read about people that were seemingly happy in their wealth and fame and then, like Robin Williams who took his own life last year --- his example at the end, showed a lack of happiness and certainly no peace. Peace could have saved him from his destruction. Now let us first address the two definitions:

<u>Happy</u>

delighted, pleased, or glad, as over a particular thing:--

Antonym [or opposite] of happy is of course the word:

<u>sad</u>----- both definitions from Dictionary.com

And then we can go to the definition of peace and its antonym

Peace:

> a state of mutual harmony between people or groups, especially in personal relations

Our personal relations would be with God as the true source of all personal relations.

Antonym for peace:

<u>insecurity</u>, ---- Dictionary.com

The opposite of peace is (of course) really in our insecurities; that we can be insecure before God, as the true Source of our insecurities. Or we can live in fear and worry about the future as another facet of our insecurities. We do not trust Him enough or we might have other things [like unresolved issues] that cause these feelings of insecurity.

Let us look at the Message translation for this peace or the more- modern term "Serenity".

> *Fear-of-God is life itself, a full life, and serene—no nasty surprises.*

---Proverbs 19:23 [MSG]

The word serene or serenity in the verse above, of course points of The Serenity Prayer which goes like this:

God grant me the serenity
To accept the things I cannot change;
Courage to change the things I can;
And wisdom to know the difference.

- *The first two lines are a prayer for peace to accept what cannot be altered in oneself ("serenity").*
- *The third line is a request for fortitude to overcome that which is possible to achieve or overcome ("courage")*
- *The fourth line is a prayer for discernment to know when to accept a situation or when to challenge it ("wisdom")*

Written by Reinhold Neibuhr (1892-1971), the prayer was widely used in sermons and Sunday school groups and studies. In the early 40s, the group Alcoholics Anonymous began to use a shortened version of the Serenity Prayer in their twelve-step program. ---Crosswalk. com

The word "serenity" is of Latin derivative and was first added to our English language in the 1500's.

With that in mind, I believe that verse really get to the heart of the matter as to the state of sereneness. This set of verses explains His grace is sufficient for me and that I can remain in this sereneness, as in the following verse:

> *And He said to me, "My grace is sufficient for you, for My strength is made perfect in weakness." Therefore most gladly I will rather boast in my infirmities, that the power of Christ may rest upon me. Therefore I take pleasure in infirmities, in reproaches, in needs, in persecutions, in distresses, for Christ's sake. For when I am weak, then I am strong.*

---2 Corinthians 12:9-10 [NKJV]

On the cover of this book, I chose to put a picture of the praying hands; everything starts with prayers, as I have found it is so true that the first part of the Serenity Prayer is what we must start with. We realize God remains Supreme in all things and all those things we cannot control we put them in His Hands, while the things we can control we ask for His directions.

Another definition of peace is here:

a state in which there is no war or fighting

- **Merriam-Webster definition for English Language learners--- online dictionary**

I think, most of us associate Peace with War or really the opposite of war.

Now for the kid's simple definition for peace we find this:

a quiet and calm state of mind

----Merriam-Webster online dictionary

Many of us older adults remember that infamous book <u>War and Peace</u> by Leo Tolstoy which we might have been assigned to read in our English classes many years ago. It can become ingrained into our minds that Peace is the opposite of War and NOT a state where you can have a lasting "a quiet and calm state of mind" as it is defined for kids in the definition above.

Most concordances suggest "a completeness" in this peace that happiness would not have. A calm assurance. A serenity that lasts. A state that only God thought Christ can provide.

It is interesting to note that the usages of Peace versus Happiness in both the Greek and Hebrews languages are altogether different. Certainly, it shows up in the usage in the NT as Christ as the Prince of Peace Who wants to share His Peace with us.

The Greek Biblical usage of this word peace is in many verses – I- RAY'-NAY [ειρήνη] -----means "figurative to be used as calm, as in still water". Or "peace as a quietness, a rest, set as one again" ----**Strong's Exhaustive Concordance of the Bible, Public Domain, published -1890**

In fact, I like to think it is the state described in Psalm 23 where "he leads me beside the still water". A quietness, a rest---a state of total serenity. Looking to Concordances and Commentaries of all the different derivatives of the Greek usage of the word Peace in the NT, I firmly believe it points to Christ as really the only one who can offer that Peace with God. Or really make us ONE with God in the end----a relative peacefulness we can realize now. So---we could say Peace is embedded in the Gospel of Christ. We really should look at this Peace He Promises as the rule, rather than as an exception to the rule. The Hebrew renderings in the OT means the word peace [in our English language] is rendered much the same in the OT.

Shortly after my son took his life, Christ caused me to remember Psalm 23 and the first few verses of that wonderful Psalm; that Psalm, by the way, had been etched in my brain at a Methodist summer Bible school that my non-Mormon grandmother insisted I go to-- some 35 years before he took his life. So naturally, I have strived to fill in the blanks by studying it for almost 24 years in what peace means to me. Picturing what it means to be totally calm and the significance of total quietness and rest.

Significantly, most of us desire this peace in our lives, along with the more modern serenity state that we can live in. I find that our Creator endowed in us that desire to achieve and live in that peace when we Believe fully in Christ. We seek not just a period where there is no turmoil in our lives but to live in a lasting sense of peace where we always trust God through that turmoil that increases trust in God; that peace is a really a natural state as opposed to living in mere happiness then back and forth between anxiety and turmoil in this fallen world we live in, that aspect of naturally desiring a peace that remains---- is laid out in Romans:

> *Therefore, having been justified by faith, we have peace with*
> *God through our Lord Jesus Christ,*

---Romans 5:1

So, let's go with Peace as a completeness or a more perfect peace—that condition of serenity that we certainly should want for our lives. And since Christ Promises that Peace {instead of happiness}, we should make it our goal to achieve Peace.

Peace I leave with you, My peace I give to you; not as the world gives do I give to you. Let not your heart be troubled, neither let it be afraid.

---John 14:27

When He uttered these words, Christ certainly knew what was about to befall Him early the next morning, yet He Promises that condition for our lives, through the Disciples at the Last Supper. The fact that He was God in flesh and would soon suffer intense physical pain from beatings and what is called "scourging" had to be on His mind. And then, certainly having his hand and feet nailed to a wooden cross. Also, to suffer the deep humiliation He would endure. Those facts are the examples of Peace we should want for our own lives. We who would desire to take on Christ in our lives should follow His example here in a True Belief in Him. We live in a crazy mixed-up world and, all too often evidenced by so many who claim to be Christians, but then a sense of this peace seems to be lacking in their lives; a lot of anger, evidential fear in their lives, frustrations and a whole lot of worry over the future. Many Christians and most certainly, non-Believers are simply following the deceptions of the world, which bring on a sense of insecurity. Many are simply seeking happiness and as I pointed out. And that aspect is so fleeting when we should seek true Peace with God.

"Lord as we strive to know about peace, I pray that my words here can at least point others to desire what is so natural and available to all who Believe in Christ. We must recognize that satan is really desiring to take our eyes off You and forget [or not even know] what it means to totally Trust in You. Help us to overcome that aspect to where our Trust in You can be complete. Help us all to learn and to picture what it means to be "beside the still water in rest' as we daily face the world and it's deceptions.

I also pray that readers can relate to my examples in some way as to finding and then living in this Peace, as it is all about your Glory. Amen"

FOREWORD

The realization that God is in control is how I would sum up this peace I have found. It is recognition of the fact that we can align ourselves with the control of God or go our way in disobedience, with a lot of worries and fear--- just like we did before we accepted Christ as our Savior. When we turn our lives over to Christ, we realize that nothing happens that God doesn't pre-ordain. He sees the bigger picture and uses our trials in life for us to gain even more faith in Him through Christ. This ultimately transforms into a trust in God. I would say gaining trust in God and receiving the peace of God are synonymous, or the two facets work hand in hand. As a Christian believer, when I look back at my life, I can see the sovereignty of God working through my past and present trials to bring me to trust in Him. While I still do make my own mistakes at times in the free will He has afforded me, but then I have tried to learn from my mistakes and more completely align myself with His Will. Ultimately, He wanted me to write about this peace that I have found. I realize that He brings me though lessons in life that ultimately makes my faith more solid. I can honestly agree with the notion the Paul writes about in Romans: "All things work together for the good of those who love God."

Yes, I have denied God a lot and gone my own way in my free will. But even then, Christ has brought me to a place where I trust His provisions of my faith more fully.

It is my prayer that readers of this book can find the trust in God as I have found, along with that blessed peace that passes all understanding. Readers can also learn how to preserve that peace because the world we live in has many ways in which it can rob us of that peace. We should at least recognize those things that may rob us of our peace, and we should know where to go to find answers.

In my testimony, which is this book, I try to point out the many ways I have found to preserve that peace now that I've found it. The world (through Satan) has many ways in which we can be robbed of that peace. I attempt to show how we can preserve the peace that passes all understanding.

INTRODUCTION

I felt the need to put in a background of sorts, leading up to the event that changed my life and brought me on the pathway where I was to become a new creation in Christ. I also want to show how utterly selfish I was for the first forty-five years of my life. Then Christ rescued me through His peace that passes all understanding, and He guarded my heart and mind, as listed in Philippians 4:7 and made me a new creation---Cor. 5:17, Galatians 5:17

At the onset of this book, I want to point to Christ from the very first, because it is about Him and what He accomplished in my life. I am simply the recipient of His grace.

I could sum up those first forty-five years of my life as a selfish, rebelling jerk. I was selfish because mostly I thought only of myself and less on the feelings of others. Certainly, I thought less about the consequences of my actions. I simply did not care most of the time. I also had a rebelling nature, because I rebelled from my father and the false church in which I was brought up. The only problem is that I took that rebelling nature to the extreme.

Calling myself a jerk is somewhat self-explanatory, and when I reflect on what motivated me in the past, with all the selfishness and all the rebelling against God, jerk describes me well.

This is not to say that now in Christ; my flesh certainly does not get the better of me at times. But faith in Christ is what I and all who claim a belief in Christ have, and we strive to live in the Spirit more fully. I spent all of my childhood and high school years as an obedient son to a dad who deeply desired for me to eventually take over our family's cattle ranch in Wyoming, which had been in our family for five generations. My great,

great grandfather cleared the sagebrush from the land and bought it from the Indians in the mid-1800s. I was the only son in my generation, but I knew early on that this ranching life was not for me. I did my best to somewhat try to please my father until I met the goal of getting out on my own by going to college. This brought on many conflicts with my dad, as well as with my mother, who brought up my four sisters and me up following the Mormon religion. I think early on when I was in my teen years; I knew something was wrong with that religion, even if I could not quite put my finger on why I had problems with it. It would take many years to discover why it was wrong and why I would eventually deny that religion which, on my mother's side, went back five generations to the times of Brigham Young.

When I left for college in 1969, I started a life rebellion against my father and the Mormon Church. I learned to drink and party; I started many years of womanizing. As I said, the drinking was my way of proving I was a jack Mormon, and I think I formally drank to that aspect many times. Occasionally at college, I even managed the time to study, and I chose a major in music because I liked to sing in high school and could (actually) sing on key.

After few years in college with a lot of drinking, I met a woman and she became pregnant. We married a few months before my daughter, Amber, was born. My new wife, Kim and I both left college and I perused a job in restaurant management to support my new family. The problem was I was not mature enough to stop my rebelling, and soon enough I was back to drinking and womanizing outside our marriage. Kim and I divorced after about three years and I then I drifted from job to job for a while. I did not take full responsibility for my young daughter until the courts caught up with me a few years later due to all the back-child support I had accumulated. I was still a selfish, rebelling jerk—with the addition of a lack of responsibility for my young daughter.

A couple of years later, I met my next wife, Darlene and then, we had two children together. I think I then gained a bit more of responsibility in that marriage, although we ended up aborting what would have been our third child in 1978 because we thought we couldn't afford another child. I believe that foolish decision we made led to a lot of problems between us. We ended up separating and then sharing our two children for the next six years until we both started to mature and tried to make our marriage work once again. The maturing process was (definitely) aided by our involvement in the Methodist Church, where I was asked to sing in their choir. It got us going to church every Sunday. I think Darlene and I realized something was missing in our lives and our marriage; - faith in God seemed to be the key.

But our growing together and learning about God was to be cut short by her untimely death in 1987 in a car accident. I was angry at God for taking my wife when we had just started to find a way to better our marriage. As things were starting to get better, I was suddenly faced with emptiness by her death. But as I learned later, it was another lesson in my life that I sorely needed.

Darlene liked to do what she referred to as 'letting her hair down' on rare occasions. One late night in October 1987, she and a friend went out partying at bars after leaving both sets of children with a babysitter. I was at work that evening, the two ended up driving along a long-stretched road where they had a single-car rollover. My wife was ejected from the car, broke her neck, and died instantly, according to the coroner. The other woman ended up with only minor injuries, and there were no witnesses to the actual accident. The highway patrolman who investigated that accident concluded that my wife was driving. I must accept his conclusions, even though there may have been more partial evidence presented to me after the fact to possibly dispute his findings. Sometimes things are not quite so clear in our lives, and then we feel we must resort to our opinions when questions remain.

From where I got off work was approximately eight miles away from the accident scene. As it turned out, God moved me to drive down that highway, not knowing what I would find. I came upon the wrecked car and my wife lying on the shoulder of the road. In the need to do something, I tried to administer CPR on her for an undetermined length of time, until the highway patrolman [who then showed up] put his hand on my shoulder and said, "It's too late" confirming what I already knew deep inside. Later that night, after I went home and told our two children what had happened with their mother; it was a unique bonding moment for us. Our children were ten and eleven when their mother died. I believe

I developed a deep resolve to do my best as a single father, for what turned out to be a three-year mourning period for myself.

Loneliness eventually got the better of me, and I started answering newspaper and magazine dating ads. God certainly was not a part of my decision to find a new wife. I eventually met and married a woman who lived across the country in New Hampshire. I moved her and her youngest daughter out to Wyoming. Her daughter went to high school along with my two children here in Wyoming. I was laid off from my job a year later, and we then we all moved back to New Hampshire, where I took on an OTR trucking job. This marriage did not last because our differences were quite severe, so my children and I moved back to Wyoming after a year and a half of living in New Hampshire. In my stubbornness, I would not give up on that marriage, and I once again moved her back to Wyoming, where we remarried. Thankfully for both of us, she moved down to Colorado to live with her daughter; we eventually divorced for the final time. I simply did not seek God's guidance before I asked her to marry me at either time. After my wife's death, I had many wonderful Christians plant many seeds in me and my two children. One wonderful Christian woman took both my children under her wing and got them involved with a Southern Baptist church. They both went to the church's summer camp, and both were saved at that camp. They went there for three summers.

I sang in the Methodist church choir, along with singing in a multi-church led by a wonderful Christian man who recently passed away. The music I was singing in those many years planted seeds in me. One wonderful Christian woman asked me to sing in her fun band, as it was called. She would play the piano while I and a couple of others would lead the nursing home residents in many Christian hymns.

This woman was instrumental in me joining the Baptist church of which I am a member for sixteen years now.

In 1994, I started going to a Church of God denomination because a man I worked with was the pastor. He and his church established more questions as to my Mormon religion, which was very much a part of me for some forty-odd years and which I had yet to deny. The true Christ was being presented to me in this church and the Methodist church, so I was still on the outside looking in as to receiving the true Christ until I was to later reject the Mormon Christ in favor of the Biblical Christ.

Then in January 1995, I was back to drinking a bit more and felt God calling me to admit myself into a Christian counseling center in California. I picked up a Christian publication handout in the entrance of the church I was going to at the time. I took it home and felt led to call the number listed for the counseling center. I found out that my work's group insurance would pay for all but two hundred dollars for this two-week stay. My two children were seventeen and eighteen at the time, and so I left them in the care of my sister and my parents, who lived nearby. I flew down to Anaheim, California, for this counseling stay. It was to be another step in the process where God was to prepare me for what would transpire just four months later. That brings me to the start of my book.

CHAPTER 1

Hitting the Very Bottom in My Life

When someone becomes a Christian, he becomes a brand-new person inside. He is not the same anymore. A new life has begun!

—2 Corinthians 5:17 (TLB)

One early summer day in 1995 started like most. There was nice sunshine, and I had some work to do in my garden. I had agreed to work with my son, Larry, later that morning rebuilding the carburetor on his car. His first car was a "big ol' boat" in the form of a 1982 Dodge station wagon and he had just added a coat of wax onto its fading finish. Fixing that car up to be roadworthy was a part of his plans to go off to a trade school in Phoenix, Arizona, later that summer, where he and his friend were moving. The two boys had already taken a trip down there the month before to check out apartments, the schools they would attend, and even places to find part-time work. They both had their plans formulated, along with the funding to start their educations and live in Phoenix. I had helped Larry out financially with a big deposit for the first semester of his trade school, and I planned to continue helping him achieve his goals.

Larry had finally found his niche' in life, his aptitudes were in computer technology. Even though it was the mid-90s at that time, when we were still somewhat in the pre-Internet age, he had already taken apart and put back together our small, personal Atari computer several times. Larry was clearly in his element when it came to computers. As he had just graduated from High School, a couple of teachers had assured me that he could go very far in that field because they too saw the excitement in him with this technology. It became a new life of learning in a field that fascinated him.

The technology has advanced so much since then, I could see him now working for some software company designing some program, or even designing hardware. I was so excited for him and proud that he was finally formulating some solid goals in a field in which I knew he would succeed. I never would have guessed what was to transpire later that morning.

When he got up that morning and made himself breakfast, I asked him about some VCR tapes (certainly some readers will remember that technology) that he agreed to copy for people at our church. That question soon turned into an argument, he left the kitchen, stormed to his room, and locked himself inside. He was my only son and given the fact that we were so similar in our demeanor, I knew we would both eventually cool down and apologize to each other. I knew he had a handgun, but suicide was not on my mind.

An hour or so later, I went to his bedroom door and asked through the door, "We okay, son?"

What ensued next was something I heard, but then, I instinctively knew what the sound was that I had heard. A large-caliber pistol going off in a closed room is very distinctive, and for most of us, we must investigate to confirm, even if what we want to confirm could potentially be horrifying or deadly. After breaking through his locked bedroom door, I gained a picture in my mind that will never be erased.

Indeed, time stands still for significant moments in our lives. A second can seem to last an eternity when from one monumental experience, a torrent of separate emotions comes into our minds. I do not think I could fully describe what a pistol to the head does when it is fired, with the traumatic carnage from a bullet entering and leaving the skull—coupled with the fact that this was my flesh and blood who was sitting there on the bed.

I don't think there was a single negative human emotion absent in me in that very moment, including a violent, physical revulsion. The picture in my mind that morning was one of physical sickness and deep horror, and certainly the ugliness of death. Now, some 24 years later, with a more completed, spiritual view--- that picture includes so much deep joy and peace, because Christ with outstretched arms is standing in that picture. From this tragedy, I found the start of peace that passes all understanding, and my trust in God is more solid. It is my deep desire to continue to learn of Him.

CHAPTER 2

Running Away

But Jonah ran away from the Lord going toward Tarshish. He went down to Joppa and found a ship which was going to Tarshish. Jonah paid money, and got on the ship to go with them, to get away from the Lord.

—Jonah 1:3 (NLV)

Running away trying to hide from it all was my first reaction after I took in the whole scene. It is in our human nature to run away from what horrifies us, or we must face a problem we cannot handle. We learn to run away from the Lord when facing our problems, as Jonah did from God's direction, as we read in the verse above. Certainly, I was initially running away from God because I didn't want to hold on to the horrifying picture of my son at that moment. Neither did I want to face the fact that as his father, I had not seen the signs beforehand of his suicide. There were a lot of whys and much self-blame in my running and hiding; I was simply running away, running toward what was familiar to me: an alcohol solution to drown it all out in my mind.

And they heard the sound of the LORD God walking in the garden in the cool of the day, and Adam and his wife hid themselves from the presence of the LORD God among the trees of the garden.

---Genesis 3:8

Adam and Eve clearly tried to hide from God the fact that they had disobeyed Him—and that Satan had deceived them. They tried to hide from God over the fact that they had clearly disobeyed God's instruction to not eat of the fruit of the tree of the knowledge of good and evil--- That is, until God confronted them.

My running away was attempting to hide through running to an alcohol solution once again that I had established from an incident in my life with my earthly father. I couldn't face God with the fact that I had failed as a father and hadn't protected the son He had given me to care for after his mother's death. I had tried to protect my son from bullying at school years before, I had tried to help him get over his mother's death; however, I failed miserably that day he took his life. I failed his sister as well, who was certainly a part of our bonding as a family. Thankfully, she was away in another town that day, so at least she was protected from what I saw. The blame, I thought, was solely on me regarding what had happened.

One other major thing I was running away from was the big question: "Where did my son go after his death?" Like many, I had heard that heaven was no place for those who took their own lives. The religion I grew up in made it very clear that suicide was a major sin and that God dealt harshly with those who took their own lives. This question ran through my mind, along with my deep guilt. For a few short moments, I was starting to suffer a major breakdown because of the horror and anguish I had just witnessed.

God does things at times in an obvious visual manner as He did for me that day. I didn't realize until months later how simple it was; He stopped me from my running. After seeing my son's death, I ran up from his basement bedroom to the front of the house toward my car. I conceivably was going to a bar for a big bottle of whiskey. But then God caused me to trip over the base of my wood stove, I hit my head, got a tiny gash, and had been effectively stopped in my running. When I got up from my fall, I was dazed a tiny bit from hitting my head on the bricks but then, the alcohol solution was no longer a desire. I started to feel a sense of comfort or peace. This was the very first time I'd received the peace that passes all understanding.

I then uttered a very basic, pleading prayer. "Lord, help me." It was a simple prayer where I was in total humbleness before Him to receive His

Grace through Jesus Christ, which is all it takes for any of us, as this verse attests to.

> *But He Therefore He says: "God resists the proud, but gives grace to the humble."*

> **---James 4:6**

I think my faith in that moment was a tiny mustard seed that was more in line with a hope that God would help me. And as it turned out, He did, even with my faith that was far from complete. I believe I was like the man who asked Jesus to cast out the demon possessing his son (Mark 8:17–26). I too essentially asked, "Lord, I believe, help my unbelief!" (Mark 8:24).

Really, that is all it takes for anyone of us: a total and complete humbleness before Christ, who will give us the Grace to overcome every situation in our lives, no matter how big or how small. I was to learn much more of this solid promise. My faith in Christ has grown these past twenty-four years. No fancy prayers, but an honest pleading for Him to come into my life with complete and total humbleness before God through Jesus Christ.

I also came upon these verses early on in my journey to find this peace.

> *Come to Me, all you who labor and are heavy laden, and I will give you rest. Take My yoke upon you and learn from Me, for I am gentle and lowly in heart, and you will find the rest for your souls. For My yoke is easy and My burden is light.*

> **---Matthew 11:28–30**

My burden was more than I could bear, and I knew that I could not face it on my own. My humble prayer was beginning to be answered at that very moment that I uttered "Lord, help me". Not realizing at the time that those exact words were used by the Gentile woman who wanted her daughter freed from demon-possession in Matthew 15:21-28. Or, very similar words of humble pleading to Him by Peter in Matthew 14:30 where he cried out "Lord, save me", when he was drowning.

Of course, turning to Him suggests a strong tower of sorts, which lines up with this notion provided by the words of David Wilkerson:

> *That is why he provided Israel with cities were set aside so that any Israelite who had overwhelming "unawares" by a problem could "run unto one of these cities that he might live."*

> ---Deuteronomy 4:42

Today we have something even better. God has provided us with a strong tower to which we can run and be helped in times of need.

> *"The Name of the Lord is a strong tower: the righteous run into it, and is safe." –*

> ---Proverbs 18:10

David in times of trouble, fled to the Rock. Jesus invites us to run under the shelter of his wings. When many of His disciples were forsaking Him, Jesus turned to the twelve and asked, "Will you run away too, like the others?" Peter answered Him, "Lord, to whom shall we go? Thou hast the words of eternal life." Peter was convinced that Jesus was the only place to hide—the only place to rest. (Excerpts from David Wilkerson's Sermon, "Why Not Just Run Away from It All?")

In my case, I was at first likely running toward an alcohol solution—from my so-called answers in the past, I could try to bury my memory that I had just established. It was a temptation to go toward what had partially worked in my past. That, which was very familiar with me: getting drunk, and this time staying that way to try to erase that horrible memory in my mind. I suppose I would have eventually died from alcohol poisoning or a disease of the liver. That was my preferred time-tested imitation solution that I, like many others have gained in our established, worldly solutions--- to not face our problems. It is all is running from the Lord and His perfect solutions.

As I mentioned earlier, part of my desire to continue my running away from God was over the abortion my wife, Darlene, and I had in 1978; It's something I tried to avoid in myself. For those who have ever gone through it [whether being a father or a mother to an aborted child], the underlying guilt truly never leaves us until we find the forgiveness through Christ for such a foolish, selfish act.

Huge issues coming from our early life can be this "running away". Rather than dealing with them, we often tend to bury them in our subconscious, desire to put them in the back of our minds, as they are too horrifying to address. We simply do not trust Christ enough to deliver His peace, the result is then we choose to hold onto these issues from our pasts. The mental health industry and the pill makers and of course, the alcohol industry are all huge recipients of these problems we try to cover up. If we trusted Christ enough to deliver to a Believer enough---we could find the real, lasting form of Peace that He is offering---if we truly Believed in Him.

CHAPTER 3

Finding the Start of Peace

And the peace of God, which surpasses all understanding, <u>will guard your hearts and minds through Christ Jesus</u>.

—**Philippians 4:7**

In the years since I have looked too many Bible verses to gain a clearer understanding of what I experienced that day. It is our human nature to sometimes dismiss things that are clearly of Christ, and maybe we do not recognize the complete gravity of a situation. We sometimes try to explain it all as mere chance or just put it away from our mind. But Christ can be in all facets of our lives, even before we come to a solid faith in Him, as my experience indicated to me. All it took for me was a complete humbleness before Him with complete submission to Him, as I later more fully established. I discovered I had a form of what we now call post-traumatic stress disorder for a few moments before Christ rescued me

"PTSD is generally caused by personally experiencing or witnessing a traumatic event. This can include a single event such as a serious accident, assault or sudden death of a loved one."

PsychGuides.com

What I experienced was (evidently) a form of PTSD, there was nothing that indicated a strength in me to have seen my flesh and blood in death and be able to handle that trauma, as well as all the guilt and questions over my son's eternal destiny. It has become so clear to me that it was all about Christ from that moment forward, how He saved me from that moment onward. The stress was simply too big for me to have handled it on my own.

"The level of stress that a person feels after losing a loved one to suicide is catastrophically high—equivalent to that of a highly traumatic concentration camp experience,"

American Psychiatric Association's "Diagnostic and Statistical Manual of Mental Disorders."

> *"In other words, if we established a "stress scale" from 0 to 100, with 100 being the highest, losing a loved one to suicide would rank at 100 – the highest stress level imaginable".*

Kevin Caruso, of Suicide.org

I do not want to make the theme of this book about suicide, but I will offer my experience and the wisdom God gave me in a later chapter. I believe I went through one of the worst traumas imaginable, and nothing else this world has offered could give me the perfect relief. Only Christ could save me. The primary theme of this book is all about Christ and the peace He has available for every one of us. The glory of my experiences belongs entirely to Him. I want to emphasize again that no supposed inner strength in me could have ever kept me from going over the edge.

In some nights afterward, I had dreams where I was overlooking a gigantic cliff, like over the Grand Canyon. Suddenly, I was falling the very long way to the bottom with increasing terror, as I saw the rocks below where I was about to splatter. Then abruptly that terror was completely erased as Christ reached out to catch me with His outstretched arms, cushioning my falling velocity. I am not one to remember most of my dreams afterward, but I do remember this one. It is a nightmare that turned out to be a very good dream. I have not had one of those dreams for many years now; I realize that even in my sleep, God was reminding me of what had happened that day. With its enormous significance in the fact that Christ rescued me that morning from the very start, after my initial temptation to run away.

*The Lord is my shepherd; I shall not want. He makes me to
lie down in green pastures; He leads me beside the still waters.*

---Psalm 23:1–2

Shortly after my son's death, while the EMTs were taking out the remains
of my son, I was led to sit on the lawn outside our house and meditate on
the still waters and green pastures of Psalm 23:2. This turned out to be
the peace Christ started right away in my mind that developed more fully
in me over the hours, days, and years ahead. It seemed immediately, as I
allowed myself to meditate on those words of that oft-quoted Psalm, a form
of peace was starting for the first time. My mind was being protected or
guarded by simply reciting Bible verses that I remembered from my youth.
If I revolved my mind to the horror I'd just witnessed, all that peace left.
The rest of that day turned to be a giant lesson, where I probably spent 6
or 7 hours until late into the night studying my Bible. Simply that peace
seemed to be more lasting through God's Word. Of course, that developed
into a pure hunger for the Word. If I did not allow my flesh to distract me
from the horror I'd just witnessed, that peace was (and now always is) there
to go back to. I also remember praying a lot that very first day, as well as
in the days to follow. In the days, weeks, months, and years after my son's
death, I guess I wanted more assurances of where his soul or spirit went;
a couple of questions kept plaguing me. "Where did my son go when he
took his life?" As I found myself being irresistibly drawn to Christ, this
next question followed the first one: "Did my son have to die for me to
start to find Christ?"

And of course, I had much self-guilt over my son's suicide. A few thousand
'what-if' scenarios worked in my mind as to the many ways I could have
done things differently. I will write more in another chapter on Christ
guarding my heart and mind through His peace from Philippians 4:7, but
I will state here that I do believe Christ brought me to the right questions
and gave me the right assurances through His Word at the right times in
order to do that 'guarding of my heart and mind'.

The morning after my son's death [a Saturday], I felt the need to go to
a Catholic Mass early, then later that day I went to my regular Church.
Evidently, the Lord had a message for me in the Catholic Church. During

the homily of the mass, the priest was speaking from Luke 23 on Christ's crucifixion. The priest seemed to look directly at me and then quoted, "Father, forgive them as they know not what they do" (verse 34). This turned out to be a message from God to me that provided a bit of trust which started on that very day, to ease my mind from all my self-guilt and the thoughts I had over my son's salvation. It was not a complete understanding, but there was a bit of comfort from the priest's message.

Later, this verse below took on some solid meanings to me over the way I should trust God over my son's salvation.

> *So, He said to them, "Assuredly, I say to you, there is no one who has left house or parents or brothers or wife or children, for the sake of the kingdom of God, who shall not receive many times more in this present time, and in the age to come eternal life."*

>   **---Luke 18:29–30**

The verse became a bit clearer as I realize that my journey in following Christ should not be inhibited by a lack of willingness to leave my children in His Care, or my son. In true application, I had to "leave" my wife who'd died eight years earlier. I needed to trust Christ even in my son's very salvation, along with my wife's salvation. It became a lesson that I was to build upon for my children, even now.

Charles Stanley suggests this about suicide in his book ***Handbook for Christian Living:***

> "With this in mind, we can understand why there are so many questions concerning whether God forgives the person who commits suicide. After all, suicide is an act of rebellion against God. Fortunately for all of us, however, God's grace is without prejudice. Whoever believes will be saved. Nowhere in the Bible does God compartmentalize sin and reserve Grace for only those who commit "acceptable" sins. There is no such thing. Does God forgive suicide? Yes, He does.

If the person who committed suicide at some time had accepted Jesus' death on the cross as payment for his sin debt and asked Him into his life, he is forgiven. Absolute assurance of forgiveness is found in Romans 8:1 "There is therefore no condemnation to those who are in Christ Jesus."

Now, twenty years later and through much Bible study and prayer, I have never found anything that suggested I might be wrong in trusting Christ on all that. I now even have more trust in Him over my son's salvation. The answer to my many prayers that Christ put in my mind initially was this: "Since you now trust Me for your salvation, why would you not trust Me for your son's?"

In the end, we do serve an awesome GOD who can snatch victory even from death. He did that very thing after all, though Christ on the cross and then through His resurrection. I was a mere recipient of Christ's perfect example.

CHAPTER 4

More of This Peace

Then He arose and rebuked the wind, and said to the sea, "Peace, be still!" And the wind ceased and there was a great calm.

—Mark 4:39

I've always liked this verse, along with the few verses before and after it. I can envision Jesus standing up in the boat— maybe holding onto the mast for balance because the boat they were in was violently being rocked by the raging storm while it was being filled with water from the fierce waves. The disciples were huddling together in fear, maybe one or two of them desperately were bailing out the water coming into the boat with each wave.

In the verses before, they were shouting out accusations to Christ because of His calmness in his sleeping. "Teacher, do you not care that we are perishing?" (Mark 4:38). A calmness or serenity from Christ seemed to indicate to them that He seemed to NOT care for their lives because drowning seemed to be their ultimate fate. Just then, Jesus suddenly wakes up, and with this same calmness and with full authority, he says, "Peace be still." Of course, the storm and the fierce waves immediately calmed, and I can even see the disciples with wild-eyed amazement at what had just happened. Jesus then said to them, "Why are you so fearful? How is it that you have no faith? And they feared exceedingly, and said to one another, "Who can this be, that even the winds and the waves obey Him!" (Mark 4:40-41). I think at that time, the disciples forgot about the storm they endured, and then they recognized that He was far more than a mere prophet—that He was God in the flesh who could control the elements of nature, just as He proved.

Scriptures do not tell us when in the night or early morning hours this particular event happened, and I like to think it happened just as the sun was rising over the Galilean mountains on a new day. As they faced the violent storm for much of the nighttime hours with increasing intensity, Christ then rebuked that storm, the clouds parted, and they were suddenly bathed in the new day's early morning light. A great calm on the waters of the Sea of Galilee. To me, it is a perfect picture of peace as only Christ can enact in our lives at any time.

This account in Mark, along with the similar accounts in the other Gospels, signifies the great calming effect Christ can have on each us in our lives. As I faced the biggest storm in my life by seeing my only son in death and all the negative emotions that came with it, Christ said to my storm and said, "Peace be still."

And of course, the account in Matthew [14:22-33] when Peter attempted to walk on water to meet Christ in this storm is highly relevant to me. Peter's request to Christ "Lord, save me!" when he was sinking because of his little faith has made an impact on my life as well.

Why am I so fearful at times? Why I have little or no faith at other times? This set of verses has been a lesson for me to remember vividly not only the storm that threatened me, but also where I was at one time in a situation where, but for the Grace of God, I was destined to drown in my sorrows. It has become a promise and a fulfilling of that promise that I hold onto. Every time a new storm comes into my life, Christ says again, "Peace be still," to that storm--that is if I listen. I can picture the clouds parting, the waves ceasing their violent actions, and a calming effect coming from Christ.

In the multi-church choir, we sang one song that I loved, "Peace Be Still." I reflected on the words and the music of the song very much in the days and months after my son's death. The song has a dramatic separation between the violence of the wind and waves of the storm, until the phrase "Peace be Still," where one can visually reflect on the stark difference with a musically enhanced calmness reflected by the words in the title of the song.

Music reflected in my mind has always been another source of peace, when I reflect on the words of Scripture in a Christian song. I suggest that for anyone as well. The hymns can add a sense of peace, especially when you are reflecting on the words of a hymn that directly quote Scripture or a promise in Scripture. It's even in a song that most of us learned as children: "Jesus loves me, this I know. For the Bible tells me so."

> **And the peace of God, which surpasses all understanding, will guard your hearts and minds through Christ Jesus.**
>
> ---Philippians 4:7

Over the years, I have found more of the solid peace described in the verse. Coupled with this next verse, the word peace has become a bedrock of sorts to my growing faith that I always find available in all discouragements and fears in my life. I have found that peace is applicable in any situations if I just look for it.

> *Finally, brethren, whatever things are true, whatever things are noble, whatever things are just, whatever things are pure, whatever things are lovely, whatever things are of good report, if there is any virtue and if there is anything praiseworthy— meditate on these things.*
>
> ---Philippians 4:8

This verse is telling us where to put our minds, or basically what we are to meditate on: whatever is true, noble, just, pure, lovely, of good report, with virtue, and praiseworthy. Learning to meditate on only these things take a lot of practice, but it is certainly achievable in growing faith in Christ.

Much is derived from the promise of the peace that Christ offers into our lives, the peace that He is ever ready to give to us when we turn to Him. For me, my former alcohol solution was to run away from God or hide from Him. My "solution" was worldly in nature and thus very imperfect—a false solution. Whether it be alcohol or drugs or any other solution we try to pretend we can find peace, it is a worldly solution that is imperfect. The true peace can only come from Christ and is listed in this verse.

> *Peace I leave with you, My peace I give to you; not as the world gives do I give to you. Let not your heart be troubled, neither let it be afraid.*

> **---John 14:27**

For non-believers, peace can be looked at as a promise that there is a solid assurance that Christ is willing and able to change one's life from constant disappointments, lack of any hope, and a life filled with so much fear over the future. If a non-believer is truly looking, he or she will see that in the lives of Believers. You will learn as I did, that the worldly solutions to finding that lasting peace in our lives are so incomplete and limited compared to what (even small faith in) Christ can do to bring us to that lasting peace. We've started to see others who may have gone through a trauma in their lives, and then Christ rescued them, as he did for me. No magical prayer is needed, nor is being in the right church where right prayers said over you. Simply put, Christ is ready to come into the life of anyone, in any place, at any time--- for those who truly humble themselves before Him at any time they cry out to Him. For me, all it took were three words: "Lord, help me," with a total humbleness before Him. He will reach people wherever they are at that moment in their lives, where the storms of life threaten to drown them.

For those of us who are believers in Him, peace adds to all this with the assurances derived from our salvation. We know the world we are living in is a temporary existence and we have the peace knowing that a glorious new life awaits us someday. A lot of peace is derived from our lives where Christ has rescued us so many times before. We have peace because He will do that rescuing again, no matter what comes our way. God allows problematic or even tragic things to happen in our lives because it builds us up to where our faith in Him is more complete.

I suggest the importance of keeping a journal. We should write down our highs and lows, our daily remembrances where we once have had our big and small problems, and then Christ's solution becomes evident. So in the months and years afterward, we can look back and see from our own words how Christ rescued us.

In our busy lives, we Believers must sometimes stop and ponder just how far God has brought us.

In the years since my son's death, I have tried to determine what exactly happened when I was delivered from a deep, traumatic experience, as well as why I was delivered from it when others have gone over the edge and lost it afterward. I read stories of soldiers suffering PTSD and looked to "psychobabble" to explain such things—all to better appreciate and then try to understand the enormous miracle that Christ performed on me.

Christ saved me from falling off that proverbial cliff, and He soon delivered to me the growing peace that remains with me to this day; that same Christ is available to all of us, no matter what our experiences or hardships in life are.

Here is a vivid example of what this peace might look like.

My son-in-law, Cory, is a captain of commercial airlines; he generally flies different aircraft for each flight. He flies for a company that provides the flight crews for the shorter routes with major airlines. He has related to me how, with all his pilot training, he has so much assurance and confidence in what he does as a career, with each aircraft he flies. He has spent so many hours in the million-dollar flight simulators, plus many hours studying training manuals for each different model of plane he might guide through the air. All of this to train him beforehand to automatically respond to all emergencies that could conceivably come up in a flight on a particular aircraft he might be flying, such as an engine fire or a loss of rudder control. He relates that as he trains on these simulators, they also have programs for each of the different airports around the country, with their peculiar wind patterns for their take-off and landing conditions. Other factors to consider are the fact that before each flight, the captain and the flight crew are notified of impending weather problems they might face in reaching their destination. They also examine maintenance logs for the individual aircraft they are flying, so that they know what to address if a problem comes up during the upcoming flight. As Cory relates it, that peace over his career leaves him on the way home in his commute from the airport, after he has landed.

In the few discussions with my Cory over his career, I have come to realize a definite form of this peace over what he does as a profession from all his training, and he passes on that peace to the passengers, usually through the cabin intercom system. This relative peace is simply from Cory's extensive training in all the potential what-if scenarios, plus knowing the aircraft he will be flying. Since my realization when I fly, I always say something to the flight crew as a word of thanks for their professionalism and training after my flight has landed. I no longer take for granted this relative form of peace that I gain during a flight.

This relative peace is perhaps an incomplete form of the peace that I write about in my book, but it is a good example. But then, the peace I have discovered covers every aspect of our lives, and it is Christ who gives that perfect peace.

In a more complete application to this peace that we can derive from studying the Bible, we have a sixty-six book training manual with a lot of simulations written into the history of God's dealings with mankind. The Old Testament is filled with examples of men and women who turned to God, trusted God, and also strayed from God at times. Why should we not study more of this "life training manual" that God provides us with? - The Bible.

Right at the beginning, Adam and Eve had one command from God. Eve let Satan deceive her to question God, and Adam followed her lead. Both partook of the forbidden fruit and were banished from the garden. They both tried to justify or explain away their disobedience to God in Genesis 3:10–13. There's so much to learn from that very first simulated experience with the whole story in Genesis, chapters 2–3. Satan is willing to lead us away from God, using our pride to accomplish a distrust of God.

Noah trusted God and had the Peace of God to build an ark and save him and his family from the upcoming Judgment by flooding the whole earth. Bible scholars tell us Noah's trust in God went on for another 120 years as he and his sons completed the ark to save them and their families from God's upcoming Judgment. I can imagine all the mocking he went through from others in those years as he was building the ark. But then, "The Lord saw the wickedness of man that was great upon the earth" (Genesis 6:5) and decided to destroy it, only Noah and his family were saved, whose faith in God remained intact for all those years while they built the ark.

Abram (later renamed Abraham), who is also listed in Genesis and then as an example in the New Testament, is pointed out as a man who trusted God and had faith in God. God told him to leave his home in Haran, along with his family, and head to the land of Canaan, not knowing what they would find. His trust in God went on to the point where he was willing to sacrifice his son, Isaac, in which he proved that he trusted God. You can find His example throughout the Bible as a man who obeyed God and trusted in Him throughout his life.

Joseph, who went through many hardships, trusted God throughout his life and ended up second in command over all of Egypt. He saved many people, along with his extended family members, from the famine that came upon the whole world. He forgave his brothers for selling him into slavery at a young age, which he later concluded that "God sent me before you to preserve life" (Genesis 45:5). He saw God's hand in it all. Not only is his story about trusting God in good and bad situations, but it is a story about forgiveness and the deep need to forgive.

Moses became the leader of Israel, and God spoke through him with the Laws God set down for the Israelites. Moses performed many miracles, where God displayed His glory and power through Moses before and during the Exodus of the Israelites from Egypt.

King David is an example of a "man who was after God's own heart." He was anointed a king over Israel by the Prophet Samuel, early on in his life. He showed his huge faith in God by defeating Goliath with a stone and his sling. The Bible tells us Goliath was well over nine feet tall, and yet David was not intimidated by the size. He realized that God was infinitely more powerful, and he trusted God to overcome this giant of a man. David had to suffer much adversity and even ran for his life for fifteen years before he was formally given the throne. He trusted God, and after many years when he has formally anointed the King. He was eventually led by his lust for Bathsheba to commit many sins. He then was convicted by God through the prophet Nathan and he is such an example of Redemption. He wrote many of the Psalms, and in Psalm 49, he laments over his sins by lusting after Bathsheba and then ordering the death of her husband, Uriah. It's a clear example of restoration to God, and we can look to Christ now as the perfect Way to receive the restoration.

There were many more prophets in the Old Testament, where God spoke through them, and their words were written and recorded throughout history.

Then in the New Testament, we have Jesus Christ, who is God's Way back to Him through His grace that He will afford to all of us. We can believe in or choose to reject Christ. The most oft-quoted verse makes it very plain as to our choice.

> *For God so loved the world that He gave His only begotten Son, that whoever believes in Him should not perish but have everlasting life.*

> **---John 3:16**

The four Gospels have their unique and individual narratives about the earthly life of God in the flesh, who emptied Himself to become as one of us. He healed the sick, opened the eyes of the blind, made the deaf hear, and even brought a few individuals back from death. Those examples are all significant because He was healing the sick, and we are all sick from our sins before we accept Christ; that He heals us through His grace and makes us well to stand before God.

> *But He was wounded for our transgressions, He was bruised for our iniquities; The chastisement for our peace was upon Him, And by His stripes we are healed.*

> **---Isaiah 53:5**

We are truly blinded by the world we live in, before Christ opens our eyes and hearts to receive Him and desire to be healed.

*The Lord opens the eyes of the blind; The Lord raises those
who are bowed down; The Lord loves the righteous.*

---Psalm 146:8

We are effectively deaf before we come to Christ and cannot receive His
Word.

*In that day the deaf shall hear the words of the book, And the
eyes of the blind shall see out of obscurity and out of darkness.*

---Isaiah 29:18

And we are dead in our sins, before Christ gives us a new life.

*Even when we were dead in trespasses, made us alive together
with Christ, by grace you have been saved.*

---Ephesians 2:5

Even we Christians are guilty of not appreciating the blessings of a
completed Bible. We, here in America, have an abundance of completed
Bibles in whatever version we can choose to make it more "readable". We
truly are those in which much has been given [Luke 12:48], with the
completed Bible in whatever form we choose to find Him. I think we often
take for granted our blessings on earth.

The Bible is our complete training manual with a lot of simulated situations
from the many men and women who lived before us and found their peace
in following God, while, of course, some did not. Through Jesus Christ,
we have that perfect way to return to God. We have free will to believe in
and accept Christ—or not. There is simply no other way.

Over the years since my son's death, I found another avenue in which
I could maintain that peace and grow in my faith --- Christian radio.
There is a translator station in remote Wyoming, broadcast in Nevada,
that I could listen to during the day and in the evenings after I got off
work. More recently we had another Christian radio station set up with

a translator tower that broadcast out of Havre, Montana. These avenue of Christian radio became a huge part of my life as they've helped me in growing my faith all those years. We simply have no excuse when we cannot find Christ in this country.

As I drove a truck over the road several years after my son took his life, another aid was the Bible on cassette tapes; technology has since gone from cassettes to CD's to iPods in the later years until now. Back then, I wore out some of those cassette tapes in my hunger for the Word because I would even go to sleep in the sleeper compartment of my truck while listening to them; a habit that goes on today with the latest digital technology, as the Word never comes back to us void. We are simply built up in our Faith the more we study the Bible in whatever form we can access it.

CHAPTER 5

Peace in Knowing that All Things Do Work Together

And we know that all things work together for good to those who love God, to those who are the called according to His purpose.

—Romans 8:28

After my wife's death in 1987, I discovered something that aided me to better be prepared in my son's death. It was something that helped me with the question, "Where is God in all this?" It is in our human nature to wonder if God took His eyes off our lives, or in this case, my son's life. Maybe God simply didn't care for a moment and let my son take his life; maybe evil won at that moment. As someone who was still not a true believer in Christ before my son's death, I prayed for my son that very morning and a short while after his suicide, I said at one time in my emotions: "This is the way you answer prayers, God? By allowing my son to take his life?"

Our emotions after a tragedy when a loved one is taken from us will go in cycles at first. I wanted to hold onto my tiny belief and trust in Him, but then I lashed out at God for a while when I took my eyes away from this peace that was slowly developing in me through Christ's grace. God has big shoulders, and as I have discovered, He allows and understands our negative emotions for a time when we lash out at Him.

The day of my son's funeral, I do believe I was further prepared to receive that peace. I remembered a few things to look for after my wife's death eight years earlier. As I struggled to see God in my situation, He showed up in His creation—or in this case, the people who displayed their comfort and love in a variety of ways.

Before my son's funeral and shortly afterward, so many had come by our house with gifts of food and some offers places to stay for family members who were coming for Larry's funeral who lived elsewhere. We received numerous sympathy cards from people who stopped by, and although they might not have known exactly what to say, they gave me and my daughter hugs in support. We also got anonymous gifts, where people did not want to identify themselves but have given their support in some small way. I suppose this is a benefit of living in a small town; the suicide of a young man brings out the love and concern for the family in many ways.

During Larry's funeral, I saw Christ reflected in a two-year-old boy. My daughter and son babysat him for a few months previously. "Geoff" grabbed a handful of Kleenex tissue and was moving from my lap and my extended family members in the first couple of rows of chairs, drying the eyes of each of us in turn. I believe most who attended were forced to smile over that gesture from a small child. God can show up in a small child in his innocence and concern, as was the case at my son's funeral with this young boy.

My sister and her husband, along with my parents, came over to my house the day after my son's death, wanting to clean up the "mess" in his room. That was a huge gesture because they felt this was our family's personal issue; all four wanted to help in this very significant way. I know God moved them in this gesture, and even on that day, I was reminded that there is a God, showing up in my extended family and, in this young boy at the funeral. Their examples were a result of being led by God to give such loving gestures. I don't think I could have handled cleaning up the mess at the time, because I certainly did not want to face the evidence of what had transpired.

This is not to say that there were no negative reactions after my son's death. I found that there was a vicious rumor going around town that I shot my son. As the rumor went on, the police were about to charge me with murder, and they were waiting until after the funeral to formally charge me. I later discovered that the rumor was generated by some boys who had bullied my son in high school. Although they felt their regrets over his suicide, they were deflecting that guilt onto me. As a suggestion to anyone, let the good coming out of people overrule the bad reactions by others. It is inevitable because some people react negatively to their guilt when a thing like a suicide happens.

After a loss, I recommend that anyone who has suffered to keep the cards as a remembrance for later to reflect upon. Gift notations in the attendance sign-in books that most funeral directors provide are aids so we can remember who to send thank you cards to and reflect upon later. I am not ashamed as a man to admit that I cried a lot when I brought out all the cards and the funeral book months and years after my son's funeral. I reflected on God's grace through His creation. I do believe tears are an aid in healing. I would like to reflect on a verse that is the shortest in the Bible in most translations.

Jesus wept.

---John 11:35

The context of this verse centers on the account of the death of Lazarus, when Mary was in deep grief over her brother, Lazarus's death. Now, even Christ, in knowing the miracle He was to soon perform in bringing Lazarus back to life, shared in Mary's grief at that moment. This verse is evidence of Christ who shares the grief in our moment of sorrow, even though He knows the bigger picture. My understanding of Christ who sheds tears along with all of us in our sorrows is augmented in other verses as well. He is ever ready to share in our sorrows, just as He did with Mary. We simply must recognize what He offers and thus believes in Him.

Christ does understand our weaknesses. From this verse, He shows He will be there with us through our trials, our temptations, and our weaknesses.

For we do not have a High Priest who cannot sympathize with our weaknesses, but was in all points tempted as we are, yet without sin.

---Hebrews 4:15

What an awesome thought, that Christ as the High Priest and in His love for us, is willing to help us face those temptations and trials we face.

In 2015, around my birthday (which was close to the twentieth anniversary of my son's death) I found something, a wonderful reminder as my son took his life two days after my birthday in 1995. Stuck in with all those cards and funeral book was a tiny, handmade card from Larry for my birthday in the year of his death. In it, he said to me through his teenaged humor, "You are a good father." It seems that little card was forgotten about and then not seen or discovered until twenty years later when we were cleaning out our garage. The tears came back to me when I found that card. I do believe God continues to bless us in our losses—and in my case, twenty years after that loss.

CHAPTER 6

Peace through Realizing God's Restoration

And the LORD restored Job's losses when he prayed for his friends. Indeed the LORD gave Job twice as much as he had before.

—Job 42:10

One unexpected aspect of learning to trust God is in what God prepared for me later after I lost a wife, then a son. I was to eventually marry a widow in 2002, who is fourteen years younger than me, and I took on three new children. The youngest boy, Casey, was four at the time.

Certainly, God had prepared me beforehand a bit more in losing my loneliness. I can remember the exact moment where I felt the huge presence of Christ in my life, and the need for a woman in my life, derived from loneliness, was never to be a factor again. I was then content in my situation as a single man who was seeking out Christ, which was exactly the lesson God had provided me in my life at the right time.

Two years after that experience, I was to meet Marti in the church we both attended; we have now been members of that church for sixteen years. In marrying her, I had many concerns and false fears. I was fifty-one at the time; taking on three new children was certainly not a goal I would ever have thought was in my future. This was coupled with the fact that Marti was many years younger. I'd lost a son to suicide, and so I had not imagined God giving me more children to care for. But as it turned out, God had prepared me beforehand to take on the role of a husband and father to these children. It was an unexpected new direction that God provided me in desiring to marry Marti. God in his directions for my life entrusted me to be a father even to more children. He provided me a lot of convincing through a lot of prayers that this was indeed what He had planned for my life. Remembering back to the convincing of God that this was indeed His direction of what He had planned for my life has served me well in the last seventeen years of our marriage. I never doubted that I had made a mistake. If we put Christ at the center of our marriage, all would go well.

"Out of the mouth of a child" innocence was certainly in Casey when at four years of age, he said, "You going to be my new dad?" He had asked this on Thanksgiving Day about two months before I popped the question to his mother. It was as if he was already convinced of it all and sensed my reluctance, the young boy turned out to be a very responsible young man who is now in his third year in college. I am truly proud to be Casey's dad.

Like Job, with God restoring to him so much, I was to receive another of these blessings of restoration. My wife and I had Jasper almost 2 years after we married; God gifted me with a total of three new sons, and God added a new daughter to boot! It is all very significant regarding the guilt I felt for not being there for Larry before his suicide, coupled with the fact that I'd failed as a father. But God would eventually entrust me with four new children. When one learns to trust God, one should not be surprised. I essentially gave my son, Larry, up to God, and He eventually restored to me four new children to love and care for. I believe He blesses us with a restoration of sorts later in life, and He does restore to us in a variety of ways when we learn to trust Him, even in our losses.

It's so wonderful that when God selects our mates, He also gives us the assurances that Christ will never leave or forsake us in or marriages; that promise has been in me for fifteen years now, and our marriage is far more solid than it was when we first married. Marti and I have taught marriage classes in our church as a couple whose perspective came from two individuals who had failed a lot in our previous marriages. We now have discovered Christ's way, putting Him in the center of our marriage.

We can relate to the many problems that come up in many other marriages, having gone through similar problems ourselves.

Certainly, Marti and I have had our ups and downs in the 17 years of our marriage. But we try to keep Christ at the center of our marriage, and He continues to bless this union. Two can become one, as we've both been reminded of at a couple of Weekend to Remember Christian Marriage retreats that we attended a few years ago; this program from Family Life has strengthened our marriage. Marti and I have been so blessed because we are endeavoring to more fully understand the aspect of two becoming one in a Christ-centered marriage. That aspect is certainly described with this verse.

> *Therefore, a man shall leave his father and mother and be joined to his wife, and they shall become one flesh.*

> **---Genesis 2:24**

As I look back at my very rich and blessed life for the past seventeen years since I married Marti and became the father of four new children, I cannot help but think God has blessed me in abundance. The following verse comes to mind as well.

> *So He said to them, "Assuredly, I say to you, there is no one who has left house or parents or brothers or wife or children, for the sake of the kingdom of God, [30] who shall not receive many times more in this present time, and in the age to come eternal life,"*

> **---Luke 18:29–30**

In my trust in God, I had to leave my deceased wife and son in His hands. Through those losses, I learned to trust Him even more through the wonderful Grace Christ has been affording me all those years since those losses. "Not my will, but Thine be done" (Luke 22:42).

When we become closer to Christ and learn to trust in Him, He does share with us through the Holy Spirit some of the ways He prepared us before we came to Him, and He continues to prepare us through our lives for new avenues where we serve Him in many ways. It is a glimpse of the bigger picture as God sees it. Regarding each piece of the puzzle in our lives from the past, by looking at them after we came to Christ, we can see a better picture of how God has been preparing us. We realize how we gained well through our trials in the past and we realize that God was working behind the scenes.

CHAPTER 7

Peace in Life versus Death

For to be carnally minded is death, but to be spiritually minded is life and peace.

—Romans 8:6

In January 2016, I had an experience where I was faced with my immortality and found the blessed peace whether I was to succumb to possible cancer—or not.

I had what was originally diagnosed as stomach flu that wasn't getting better after a few days. I eventually went to an Urgent Care, a walk-in medical clinic that is also open on weekends where they initially confirmed the stomach flu diagnosis but did blood tests then, sent me to get prescriptions for this supposed stomach flu. While waiting at the pharmacy to have my prescriptions filled, I got a call from the clinic, was told that I needed to get to the ER of the hospital immediately. The blood tests indicated that I had a severe case of pancreatitis and very likely Cancer as the cells had shown up.

After relating that message to my wife, Marti, she told me that was exactly what her deceased former husband was diagnosed with before he eventually succumbed to cancer in 1999. Our anxiety heightened. We uttered a quick prayer together as she rushed me to the ER of the hospital.

The doctors had a bit of problem coming up with a firm diagnosis. I had an operation in my lower abdomen forty years before, which was somewhat masking the problems. But even then, Christ was guarding my heart and mind, as well as Marti's (Philippians 4:7), due to our simple prayer. The surgeon was called in and ordered an emergency operation for me the next morning, telling me he did not know what he would find other than my gall bladder that looked as if it needed to be removed. He was concerned about Cancer as it was still a big possibility. I do not remember one anxious moment where I was particularly concerned over what the doctors would find. While lying on the gurney early the next morning before I was taken in for surgery, I had the peace of God flooding me. I knew I did not have any big regrets in life, and certainly, my wife and children would be taken care of. The song "His Eye Is on the Sparrow, and I Know He Watches Me" continually played in my mind until I went under from the effects of the narcotics, they had given me. The lyrics somewhat center around this verse:

> *But the very hairs of your head are all numbered. Do not fear therefore; you are of more value than many sparrows.*

---Luke 12:7

When I woke up from surgery later that morning, the first person I saw was the surgeon, who told me, "Jim, it was just your gall bladder, which we removed. No cancer of any form."

My wife soon learned of the news, and we gave our praises to God that He had spared me.

I feel my peace from God has essentially been completed in a sense because through the issue of my life-or-death wonderment, I found it even then. Now I want to present that peace to all who lack it in their own lives. From Philippians 4:7, "Christ will guard our hearts and minds through this Peace" if we firmly place our trust in Him. Through our humble "prayers and petitions," He will grant us that peace because we know He is watching over us when we truly believe in and trust Him.

> *You will keep in perfect peace all who trust in you, all whose thoughts are fixed on you*

---Isaiah 28:3

That perfect peace is such a blessing that I can always go back to and reestablish where you can fully trust God even in life versus death; if He decides I must leave this earth tomorrow, I am ready.

CHAPTER 8

Peace over Our Children

*Evil people will surely be punished, but the children of the
godly will go free.*

—Proverbs 11:21 (NLT)

Marti and I have six children combined. Five are out on their own, and
we have Jasper still at home as a freshman in High School. Of course, I
lost another son as well.

There have been lots of ups and downs with them, but I believe the Lord
has given me a peace over them and the choices they make in their lives,
coupled with the fact that all have been grounded in Christ Jesus. I always
must go back to the lesson I learned with my deceased son, which is
turning them over to God and trusting in Him.

My daughter Dawn, who lost her brother in 1995 and her mother in 1978,
has been an example to me of how I, as a father, can better be there for
her even after she left home after graduating from high school. I trusted
in God for her future. She ran from God for many years after she lost
her brother; for a while I believe she somewhat blamed me for his death,
along with her blaming God. She also didn't have any good memories of
her deceased mother as she confessed. As my faith in Christ grew, I wrote
her many letters over the years about the peace I felt through Christ, with
memories of her mother that I had. I helped her recognized her mother
as a very special person, but just as immature as I was back then. I made
many prayers over my daughter, Dawn, all these years, and I believe God
protected her in her running from Him. He eventually brought her back to
Christ about two years ago; this was significant, her goal was always to get

married and start a family. We both agree she was finally ready; she was at the point in her life where all the anger and bitterness had been removed by Christ. Her renewed faith in Christ was growing. In 2015, she finally met the man God had prepared for her; she went on to marry him. I had the honor to give her away as a father in their wedding ceremony in Colorado.

I turned my daughter over to God, as well as my son who took his life. I believe that aspect can work for all parents whose children are adults and on their own. My added aspect there with Dawn was to always think of her, call occasionally, and write many letters.

Maybe I am old-fashioned, but I do believe a hand-written letter is far more personal. When we write to encourage, using Bible verses and about Jesus Christ as I did all those years, I believe it encourages the recipient (and us). In this technology-savvy world, the aspect of sitting down and writing a letter is the best form of communication; I recommend it to anyone. It has been a blessing for my life as I have found the Word never comes back to us void. That is, I do believe when we share God's Word, it tends to encourage us as well in our sharing. Over the last twenty years, the list of people I write to regularly has grown, including two prisoners. I will admit as my penmanship got slowly worse, I then adapted writing a letter on my computer.

Right now, our two younger adult children have somewhat left the Christian faith. Our youngest daughter is studying anthropology and sociology, and has adopted a lot of evolutionary theories. She and I have had a few debates over that, but I still maintain a peace that God has it all in control. Her mother and I must turn her over to Him; it will not be us who brings her back to the Christian faith, but God. There must be an *if* in all that. We should not put up walls against her due to our disagreements about Christ. We must simply point out how proud we are of her achievements over the last four years in her college education, and how well she has done in all that. We are keeping those lines of communication open, I write letters to her about Christ without preaching, as well as her mother talking to her a lot on the phone.

This wonderful young lady called me up the day after my surgery in January 2016 told me how much she appreciated me as a father for the last 15 years of her life. I believe her mother related how potentially serious my operation was. When we feel blessed, these moments are memories to cherish always. I am truly rich beyond measure as to her appreciating me as a father who took over after the death of her biological father; I have never had any regrets in adopting three new children in my marriage to Marti. I also got a call that day from the older son with much the same appreciation; I will never forget what was said by both.

We all must give our adult children up to God and keep the communication aspect very open, as Christ-believing parents. We must learn to accept but not always endorse their individual choices in lives, if they have left what they were grounded within their Christian faith. Our two younger adult children are going through their belief-system differences right now, but with my trust in God, I must always go back to the fact that I have turned them over to Him. Our son Casey, who is now in his junior year in college, and I have had many father-son conversions that invariably end up discussing matters of faith. I see him now as someone who has explored the different belief systems (including atheism), and God could make him a great apologist for the Christian faith; but I must trust in God on all that.

I believe we worry about our adult children sometimes needlessly. We should always pray for them, but we must trust God on their journeys in life. I know for me, like all my children before, they have decided at one time to accept Christ in their lives. Although we wish that they would live their lives in accordance with their faith, it doesn't always work out that way.

This part of peace over our children, especially after they have reached adulthood is essential. Right now, as I write this portion of this book, Marti and I have our oldest son [Mat] who is having a huge problem with alcohol. He lost his job, cannot drive because of a DUI and has mounted up huge hospital bills. We took him into our home eight months ago, after his Clinical Abuse Treatment of three months. Before that, he almost died in a hospital; his liver was starting to shut down from his binge drinking. Unless we took him in, he would be one of the homeless. The Lord is slowly providing answers, part of my challenge had been to be patient and remember the times I went through rebellion many years before. We pray for him constantly as he is essentially doing his running away from God. We simply have to Trust God that He will turn his life around in God's timeframe. As of this moment, he is back at another Treatment Facility, but then he is starting to realize his problems which stem from a lack of hope. Once again, I am writing him long letters to him about the Source of this Hope that he can find.

CHAPTER 9

Peace through Learning to Resist A Conformity to the World

And do not be conformed to this world, but be transformed by the renewing of your mind, that you may prove what is that good and acceptable and perfect will of God.

—Romans 12:2

One aspect I've discovered to help me preserve God's peace is in the areas where I allow in myself these little conformities to the world that divert my attention from this peace. The world around us in American society, [which I of course, live in] has a lot of Me First people in it and a lot of "buy more, do more, see more, experience more, and be more" attitude that infect all of us as believers, whether a little or a lot. Marketing is aimed toward the lusts we can be deceived by, for all the things we think we must have to supposedly make our lives richer and supposedly fuller to fill our lives with happiness for a moment. This goes along with the peace we think we can gain by having more worldly possessions, versus the real peace through Christ. As my wife and I are discovering, we need to have a solid distinction between what would be considered a necessity versus a luxury. The world's marketing powers are very much around us.

A good example of the powers of marketing was when my son Larry and my daughter Dawn were growing up around the time McDonald's restaurants were becoming a huge force in America. Their barrage of television ads then was filling our children's minds with pictures of the golden arches, and Ronald McDonald the clown was making appearances in their restaurants. I do believe my daughter Dawn could say "Donalds" and pick out the golden arches from two blocks away while we were driving before she could say, Mommy or Daddy. We had set our children before the television for much of the day, with its countless commercials on all the cartoon programming; that same example of the marketing forces is very problematic in us adults as well, and over the years I have done my fair share of impulse buying—a lot from just walking into a home improvement store, for example. Now, as a new creation in Christ, I have realized that this subtle conformity generated by the world around us is very powerful in deceiving. When Marti and I married, canceling our cable television programming was one of the first things we did because our children were mesmerized by watching it all, along with the constant barrage of commercials aimed toward their childlike greed to plead for new toys and games. Now, we have computer streaming, but we can control it a bit better for our 15-year-old son.

Coupled with the fact that the content of television programming has gone so far downward (where what would be a PG-13 rating now would be considered an R rating thirty years ago) is the fact that we have let the huge force of commercialization come into our homes. Our television viewing habits can be a double-edged sword. We should be concerned about the content of the television programs we or our children watch, but we should also be concerned by the commercials that tempt us with our lusts to buy more, do more, and have more. It simply became more evident in my older children thirty years ago that we can adapt conformity to the world, which in turn robs us of our peace through Christ, or at least take our eyes off the perfect peace.

In this computer age, where we now have pop-up ads to get us to buy more stuff, it is a constant challenge to resist that temptation to accumulate more possessions that supposedly enriches our lives by more buying. I believe the conditions of the perilous times of the Last Days, as described in Paul's second letter to Timothy, are all around us in abundance.

> *But know this, that in the last days perilous times will come:*
> *For men will be lovers of themselves, lovers of money, boasters,*
> *proud, blasphemers, disobedient to parents, unthankful,*
> *unholy, unloving, unforgiving, slanderers, without*

self-control, brutal, despisers of good, traitors, headstrong, haughty, lovers of pleasure rather than lovers of God, having a form of godliness but denying its power. And from such people turn away!

---2 Timothy 3:1–5

We can see countless examples of each of these "conditions of men" around us in such abundance, and we can develop relative conformity to these conditions as Believers and end up wanting what they want. That the last days are already here with these conditions and a True Believer should want to eliminate following along. We Believers should adopt a form of humbleness and realize how many of those conditions might apply to us.

CHAPTER 10

Peace through Forgiveness

But if you do not forgive, neither will your Father in heaven forgive your trespasses.

---Mark 11:26

This verse points to the part of the Lord's Prayer where we say we forgive others for their trespasses as we are forgiven by God. It's a two-part thing because to be forgiven, we must forgive others. And in the application, we might carry burdens in our lives until we have forgiven others for the many things we have experienced in our past. Of course, forgiveness for ourselves is something we have to accept from Christ.

My two-week stay in the counseling center in California a few months before my son took his life was to be a seed of learning the aspect of forgiveness that God gave me, it increased for many years afterward.

I do believe my earthly father and his frustration over me as a young boy was the primary root of my need for forgiveness of others. As I learned to forgive my father, other things from my past and who did what to me were far easier to gain regarding this forgiveness. A true humbleness before God makes us realize that we should hope others we have wronged will forgive us as well, especially in my being a selfish, rebelling jerk for so many years before I came to Christ.

As I mentioned earlier, I was not cut out to take over my father's ranch, yet my dad certainly wanted it to be that way because I was the only boy in my generation. I discovered that I had one repressed memory of my father beating me unmercifully in front of my friends and other adults when I was thirteen or fourteen. This was the start of my solid rebellion against him, which went on for some thirty years. By humbly knowing my frustration and realizing how I handled it all as an adult myself, I was essentially copying my father's frustration and anger for many years. Humbly realizing I needed forgiveness for myself over my many displays of anger and frustration toward my children and my deceased wife when I became an adult made it easy for me to find forgiveness for my dad. We do copy our parents' good and bad examples, whether we do realize that fact or not.

At the counseling center, they used an example; a group setting where fifteen of us sat around in a circle. We were instructed to pass around a Styrofoam cup, where we tore out a page of a big LA phone book, wadded it up, stuffed it inside the cup. As you can guess, the cup ended up bursting down the sides after the tenth person shoved in a wadded-up page. This is precisely what goes on when we have all this unforgiveness toward others. We end up having this junk inside us, and nothing is ever resolved or let free by Christ. We burst out in anger and frustration because of all this junk inside us, as we create in ourselves a condition where we cannot handle one more piece of junk. I knew many in that counseling center at the time I was there had far worse situations in their lives; some that had been sexually abused as children. The aspect is still the same; that is a concept in learning how to forgive. You notice people have gone through worse situations in their lives; you must reflect on all the people you have hurt yourself. The pain from our pasts almost seems insignificant compared to, (for instance) a woman who had been sexually abused as a child, or a young man who had witnessed his mother's murder as a child.

Corrie Ten Boom, the author of the book _The Hiding Place_, uses as one of her examples, - awesome power of forgiveness from and through Christ. After her message on forgiveness in a church service, she was confronted by a former German SS guard who was one of her jailers during World War II. As she relates, "As I took his hand the most incredible thing happened. From my shoulder along my arm, a current seemed to pass from me to him, while into my heart sprang a love for this stranger that almost overwhelmed me." She knew she needed to truly forgive that man for the horrors she went through many years earlier, and she gave a simple prayer:

"Lord Jesus, forgive me and help me to forgive him." At that point, she and the former SS guard were equal; they both needed Christ's forgiveness.

What an awesome power Christ offers us in simply forgiving others who have wronged us. Only Christ can grant us that ability to forgive and thus set us free and give us a vital aspect of the peace from His removing all that junk that is inside us.

As to my dad, I was rewarded with closeness to him that I never had for the last eight or nine years before he passed on. I forgave him for my childhood experiences. I was to hold his hand in the last few hours of his life and assure him that I would take care of Mom before he succumbed to cancer raging through his body. Along with my oldest daughter, Amber, I told him about the True Christ through reading many Scripture verses and through a lot of prayers over him. A few months before that, I felt led to write him a long letter on all the good aspects he gave me while I was growing up. We had many good, long talks in those final years; I found the forgiveness towards him through Christ. We enjoyed our new father-son relationship before he passed away in 2005 and of course, part of our renewed relationship was based on Christ and the Bible.. Adding to this, was the fact that 20 years earlier I was the one who baptized him into that Mormon Church. Later with the True Christ, God allowed me to share in pointing him in the right direction. Part of the Hope I have in God, is the fact you do not know when He will use you for to share His Glory. I have the assurance of his salvation, because I did my part in essentially planting the seeds and it is up to God for the increase—1 Cor, 3:6, 7

The other huge aspect for me regarding forgiveness was toward the other woman who was with my wife the night she died. I admit that my opinions (derived from my questions over the accident) resulted in me to blame who likely was driving at the time of the accident. Certainly, forgiveness for myself was a huge factor over aborting what would have been our third child with Darlene in 1977. It is amazing the grace Christ has afforded; not only did He forgive me but He let me find forgiveness for myself over it all. And of course the "Proof" there was the fact that God entrusted me to raise 4 new children in His new direction for my life.

I found more of the blessed peace from Christ by forgiving this woman, my father, and myself, as well as everyone in my past who hurt me in some way; I believe I carried around a burden for most of my life. Christ promises us freedom, and freedom is a solid release from our lack-of-forgiveness burdens.

> *Stand fast therefore in the liberty by which Christ has made us free,¹ and do not be entangled again with a yoke of bondage.*

---Galatians 5:1

This verse refers to the bondage of sin we carry around before we come to Christ, but it also refers to the freedom He affords us when we find forgiveness for others who have hurt or wronged us—and for ourselves. As Mark 11:26 tells us, we must forgive in order to be forgiven and thus enjoy this freedom. Christ will make us completely free if we turn over all our cares and woes over to Him. He is the great healer.

CHAPTER 11

Peace despite Politics

Beware lest anyone cheat you through philosophy and empty deceit, according to the tradition of men, according to the basic principles of the world, and not according to Christ.

—Colossians 2:8

Currently, now in August of 2019, we are a Nation under a President who has been in office for over two years and very controversial. Many Christians, including the proclaimed Evangelicals, have made him fit prophecies in the Bible including the notion that makes him not unlike King Cyrus, listed in 2 Chronicles and other Books of the OT. They even have a coin minted with his image superimposed over a rendering of King Cyrus. As if God wants us to make an idol of any man and buy an actual coin depicting that idolatry. This all is reminiscent to when Moses came down from the mountain with the Ten Commandments and found the Israelites had made an idol of a golden calf. This whole issue was started by a few Jewish rabbis and if one notes, the traditional Jewish Faith does not recognize the NT and its prophecies from Christ about these Last Days.

Many are simply being cheated by this philosophy empty deceit of man [in the world we live in] and not according to Christ, Who we all should seek as Believers.

And of course, the driving force in politics is all the special interest groups and their huge infusions of money to finance the candidates who will best serve their interests. Segments of the population are being guided by these issue ads that best serve their individual needs and pretend to claim to eliminate the fears we can sometimes adopt. We are at the brink of collapse in this country because so little that has come out in the campaigns in the last few years that can be construed as truth, or real truth----that has no attached bias.

I do believe God is turning us over as a nation to our own devices. As the adage goes, "We don't elect the politicians that we think we want, but the politicians that we deserve." We might be in for a very bumpy ride in the next few years because things could get conceivably worse.

As Christians, we try to falsely combine our Christian ideals and the worldly nature of politics, as if voting for or against a candidate might be how we think God would want us to vote. Many simply adopt the false rhetoric coming out of the campaigns and the political pundits as if some politicians are speaking from God. Like the nonbelievers, we adopt the fears garnered by the talking heads we want to listen to, even disdain or adopt hatred toward candidates on the opposing side.

I am not claiming to be an eschatologist, but I do believe some of the signs of the Last Days are here now as they have been for two thousand years since Christ walked the earth. Just before the rise of the antichrist or the conditions of the "Force of the anti-Christ" come forward, we are not suddenly going to find ourselves in brand-new conditions, such as those listed in the many prophesies of the Last Days. Those conditions will always be present and at times [like now] will intensify.

When asked about the signs of the Last Days by His apostles in the Olivet Discourse in Matthew 24, Christ stated very significantly in verse 4 by saying, "Take heed that no one deceives you." That's a very clear warning that deception will be tantamount now just as it has been a force throughout history and that deception is more perverse right now. His warning at the very first of this discourse is a major warning of something to resist as things get worse. We Christians are allowing and even adopting into our own lives a lot of worldly deception through the political forces, led by the moneyed interests, to get us to vote one way or another. Lots of false prophets tell us to be very fearful if the opposing candidate is elected; they state what their candidate will do to turn around this nation. As listed in Matthew 24:11, they will "deceive many."

That is why I always go to this verse:

Test all things; hold fast what is good.

---1 Thessalonians 5:21

In the 2nd Book of Thessalonians we find this set of verses of course:

*The coming of the lawless one is according to the working of Satan, with all power, signs, **and lying wonders**, and with all unrighteous deception among those who perish, **because they did not receive the love of the truth**, that they might be saved. And for this reason, God will send them strong delusion, that they should believe the lie.*

----2 Thessalonians 2:9–11

To my Evangelical friends with their avid support for this President; how do these set of verses work considering all the mistruths and outright lies our President has uttered through, mainly his Tweets?

I believe when we pay more attention to politics and go to our one-sided sources for "truth", it tends to unsettle us, can cause us to fear, and we even adopt hatred for others with opposing viewpoints. Many of us are looking for relative truths. In periods of my life where I paid more attention to politics and not to "whatever things are of good report" (Philippians 4:8), I tend to get more agitated. We simply must gain a love of truth in all forms and rely less on our worldly-generated opinions, which are so often misguided.

A few months ago I picked up a copy of *Time Magazine* which I do not normally read. On the cover, it said, "Is Truth Dead?" It got me to thinking that even the editors of a secular magazine are sensing there is something wrong, particularly in a political fashion, where truth is only relative.

What we have is a condition where the world has set up its many deceptions via our political discourses; many political commentators do not the love of truth or all truth in giving their analysis of the News. As a Christian believer, one must separate what is of God and what is of the world via our political discourses; we make those lines of separation distinct. There is an underlying indoctrination (via the world) going on, centered around politics where people on both sides of the political divide are espousing their truths - not necessarily God's truth.

In this world around me, I ponder on these verses, as well as the teachers we often set up to tell us what we want to hear politically.

> *For the time will come when they will not endure sound doctrine, but according to their own desires, because they have itching ears, they will heap up for themselves teachers; and they will turn their ears away from the truth, and be turned aside to fables.*

> **---2 Timothy 4:3–4**

No, these very biased political commentators are not teaching doctrine per se, but they are leading people astray in their application of the sound doctrine. Often people collectively hear what they want to hear, the truth is based on what people want to believe according to their political biases.

We simply must remember God is very much in control, in the last few elections that fact is more evident. "Not according to Christ" is the way I must look at the political atmosphere in this country. I really must follow the directives of this verse regarding how I look at politics, the clear and obvious deceptions in worldly politics.

> *And He said to them, "Render therefore to Caesar the things that are Caesar's, and to God the things that are God's."*

> **---Luke 20:25**

When asked about paying taxes, Jesus essentially replied that Caesar represented the world we live in, "Render to Caesar what is Caesar's" That is far different than the God we are supposed to render our Worship. Our allegiance to Caesar (in the form of politicians and the political parties they represent) should be far different than the "things that are God's."

I believe for the peace I try to maintain I try to look in Independent sources for my news. One wants to stay somewhat informed, but one must recognize that in this world there are so many biases in our news. One will get unsettled or even angry when one follows and believes in a form of bias from the political debates and then, lose the sense that God ultimately is in control.

CHAPTER 12

Suicide (or the Lack of Hope as the Cause)

For we are aliens and pilgrims before You, As were all our fathers; Our days on earth are as a shadow, And without hope.

—1 Chronicles 29:3

In the past few years, I have tried to determine why my son took his life. Why did he do what he did? What was the common element that led to his suicide? What element contributed to his lack of hope and peace in the final moments of his life, and what pushed him over the edge?

Two aspects I have determined is that Larry did not want to exist without his mother. Her impact on his life was huge, and when she was taken from us, he didn't want to go on with life without her. I saw a lot of signs shortly after his funeral from his secular counselor and others who knew him that indicated there was a side to him that wasn't so readily seen. Certainly, the aspects of his being bullied in school contributed to it. These two elements pushed him over the edge with increasing intensity. A good analysis is this one.

> "A major cause of suicide is the despair of living without meaning or purpose. In a world overwhelmed with violence, divorce, homelessness, disease, and drug abuse, it is often the norm to live life bouncing around without anything to hold onto that would give meaning or security to an otherwise lonely existence.

The fact that many children are finding suicide to be logical choice underscores the impact that the pressures of life, even at an early age, can have. They live a world of isolation, rejection and the perception that no one cares. Life becomes intolerable, and suicide is the "logical" answer. Depression is the key factor in most suicides". --- ***Charles Stanley's Handbook for Christians Living***

Clearly, there is no visible hope without Christ for many of our nation's youths, and adults as well. I often think about what an impact we Christians could have if each of us were to mentor one child, not in our immediate families. This lack of hopelessness in our nation would be significantly reduced by Christians reaching out and sharing their faith. Planting seeds particularly in our youth in this country would provide them with an alternative to this lack of hope. We are trying to come up with all these government "solutions" to curb the suicide rates, but we each should try to take care of our tiny corners of the world.

The ideal is that we who are Believers must be "salt and light" to the unbelieving world—a world filled with violence, hopelessness, and despair. We, who have found the trust and hope in our salvation in God, are not doing a very good job of reaching out to those who are filled with a lack of hope.

> *And are confident that you yourself are a guide to the blind,*
> *a light to those who are in darkness.*

---Romans 2:19

This applies not only to our youth, where many have adopted a sense of hopelessness but to all who we meet in a chance encounter. The light we have in Christ needs to be shared in a world filled with so much hopelessness.

The number of Christians in America has held steadily at 73 percent, according to Barna Research; with such a clear majority of people who profess a faith in Jesus Christ, why is there such a clear lack of hope? I think the above article from *Charles Stanley's Handbook on Christian Living* can be summed up as a lack of solid hope that comes through Jesus Christ and is depicted in this verse.

> *Now hope does not disappoint, because the love of God has been poured out in our hearts by the Holy Spirit who was given to us.*

> **---Romans 5:5**

My thoughts are that we, as believers in Christ, should be sharing more of this peace and hope to a world filled with despair; a clear lack of hope. We, believers in Christ have the awesome power to deliver hope to others through the light of Christ, which we were given. I pray for an Awakening in this country, as well as in other countries around the world, that there is an answer to that lack of hope in so many, which is Jesus Christ and the peace He can give us when we trust in Him.

CHAPTER 13

Peace of God versus Peace with God

"There is no peace," says the LORD, "for the wicked."

—Isaiah 48:22

One aspect of coming to true faith in Christ is realizing that we before we accepted Christ are the "wicked" in this verse. We need a Savior because "all have sinned and fall short of the glory of God" (Romans 3:23). That is why God offers us His only begotten Son as a Savior to achieve the "everlasting life" in the following verse.

> *For God so loved the world that He gave His only begotten Son, that whoever believes in Him should not perish but have everlasting life.*

---John 3:16

In God's love for us, He offered Christ to pay the penalty for our sins. You simply cannot have the PEACE **OF** GOD unless you address the questions: "Have I made peace **WITH** God? Have I accepted that Jesus is my Savior, and do I truly believe in Him? Have I addressed the fact that as a sinner I need a Savior?"

> **Therefore, having been justified by faith**, we have **peace with God** through our Lord Jesus Christ,

---Romans 5:1

The verse above simply adds the "Justified by faith" qualification to having this peace. Once we have met that step of course, then we can have the PEACE OF GOD as this verse points out:

> And let the **peace of God** rule in your hearts, to which also you were called in one body; and be thankful.

> ---**Colossians 3:15**

We must truly humble ourselves before God, just as I did when I said the simple prayer of "Lord, help me" on the day my son took his life. I was truly at a place in my life where the alternative solution didn't look good, and I was tired of running. His grace effectively caught me from running away, and it truly humbled me.

> *But he giveth more grace. Wherefore he saith, God resisteth the proud, but giveth grace unto the humble.*

> ---**James 4:6**

- This theme of "humbleness before God" is throughout the Bible: James 4:6, Psalm 138:6, Proverbs 3:34, and 1 Peter 5:5 as well as many other places. That aspect was the turning point in my life, where I offered up the simple prayer of "Lord, help me." I was drawn toward these feeling of calmness, and I discovered more by simply reading His Word. I saw myself as a sinner in a desperate need of a Savior. I effectively needed the gospel of Christ in my life.

The gospel of Christ can be summed up in four very vital steps.

- **Who are we accountable to?----- God.**
- **What is our problem?--- Sin (through Adam) that separates us from God.**
- **What is God's perfect solution to our problem?--- Jesus Christ.**
- **What is my decision?---- To realize a Faith in Christ, and to turn to and follow Him**

The first step in the process is the hardest to realize. Unless we humble ourselves before God and realize the absolute need for God's perfect solution, we cannot believe in the completed Gospel of Christ.

I truly believe that finding faith in the completed gospel of Christ, which is essentially summed up here in this verse.

> *And the peace of God, which surpasses all understanding, will guard your hearts and minds through Christ Jesus.*

> **---Philippians 4:7**

The peace of God is firmly established through our trust in Him and though His promises to us.

CHAPTER 14

Peace in Our Health

You will keep him in perfect peace, Whose mind is stayed on You, because he trusts in You.

—Isaiah 26:3

It is so telling that Isaiah in his prophecies told of a Jesus Christ, Who was to come in so many verses. This is the theme that we should adopt in this New Testament era "perfect peace as long as our minds and our trust stay [with Christ]"

In my effort for an example of that is, midway through writing this book I suffered a minor stroke; it was not a major stroke in which one side of my body would have been affected permanently but it was one where my balance was problematic for a short time afterward. Then, putting thoughts together as I once could was another problem. An MRI showed a bit of brain damage, I had to learn again how to comprehend by essentially rerouting my thought process because of that brain damage for about two months; I lost my confidence that I could finish this book and have normal comprehension. But then I remembered thinking one day, [when I learned to put my thoughts together] "Why not apply this trust in God that I have developed? As I prayed to God to help me in this endeavor to essentially reroute my brain, that peace flooded me as it had in so many other situations in my life. As I discovered, the brain is a marvelous thing because it can reroute itself despite the dead areas that come from a stroke. To me, it is another proof of the existence of God who gifted us all with a brain we can use. To me, it is ludicrous to think that such a marvelous instrument as our brain could have evolved someway. Unless there is huge damage to the brain, He will provide a way for us to get back to a relatively normal state and once again find that Trust in Him that we had established before.

This is another thing I can rejoice in [Phil. 4:4] as I believe my Faith is enhanced even more since my stroke. Even though God used my stroke to convince me to retire, I am now able to concentrate more fully on Him and the Words of the Bible.

Our former pastor's grandson was born with a condition called cerebellar hypoplasia, which is a condition from an underdeveloped brain in the womb. When it was first discovered, "Josiah" would likely not be able to walk or function as a normal boy, according to the medical specialists. Today, some ten years later, he not only can walk and run, but he has mastered the art of learning. He is now an 8th grader in our school system; of course, his family never told him he was disabled but encouraged him through his trials. His example has been a great inspiration for me.

My niece, Teri, has been another inspiration to me. She has been in a wheelchair for over twenty years. Her spinal cord was compressed due to a falling accident. She has never walked and suffered a lot of pain. She even drives her van with hand controls to and from work and church. She has remained a Christian all these years, despite the severe pain that comes with her condition, she trusts in the Lord. Recently she has received an experimental drug that is supposed to relieve the pain without having to rely on heavy narcotics; we are all praying that the drug will do what it is supposed to do.

My neighbor's son, Bruce, who has had Spinal Bifida since birth and has never walked in his life, has been another inspiration for me. He is now almost 60 years of age and gets around town in his wheelchair. Nothing seems to trouble him.

We can all find situations where people are suffering a lot worse than we are. Christ opens our eyes and shows us that others are enduring while keeping their faith in Christ.

And when we look back and see God at work through our Tribulations, we end up Trusting Him more.

I must say that in my life I have found that any kind of drug [prescription or otherwise] inhibits the Holy Spirit in me. God has given me a low tolerance to prescription drugs [including painkillers] and I pray that I will continue in this fashion as I get ever older and particularly arthritis sets in more.

There are many pieces of evidence of the drug industry's marketing to where people have been "hooked" on painkillers; when the prescriptions run out, they must go to other means for drugs because they got addicted - to keep me very wary. I simply have learned to Trust God on any pain issues in my life and to continue that Trust IF I get a new pain.

CHAPTER 15

Trusting in the Sovereignty of God

Trust in the Lord with all your heart,
and lean not own understanding;
In all your ways acknowledge Him,
And He shall direct your paths.

—Proverbs 3:5–6

At some point in a true believer's life, one must acknowledge that God is ultimately in control. He allows things to happen to us, and there is no apparent answer at the time of our trials. He does, however, sometimes give us clues later as to the why particular circumstances happened in our lives. We realize later a blessing from a particular lesson that happened to us. It happened to teach us this much-needed lesson and ultimately to bring Him glory. Other Christian authors refer to it as the Providence of God, but I do believe it means much the same thing. God ultimately allows certain things to happen in believers' lives in His sovereign will.

When I find myself trying to "lean on my own understanding" and not ultimately trusting in Him, this is where real perplexity enters along with a lot of human blame, and anger; resentment surfaces and false or incomplete judgments. A lot of things can ultimately take us away from God and trusting in Him and threaten our Peace.

For almost thirty years, I have unanswered questions as to the night my former wife died and the woman who was with her that night. It was not as clear as I would have liked in my understanding of the incident, but now those answers I once sought are no longer relevant. Ultimately, we have to accept and trust in God's Providence.

I read the account of Timothy McVeigh's execution a few years ago. He was the Oklahoma City bomber who was convicted of blowing up a part of the Murrah Building killing 168 people in 1995. Family members who lost loved ones, who also witnessed his execution claimed that there was not the closure that they had hoped for after his execution. That real closure can only come from God and trusting His providence when we lose loved ones.

As to my grief, it has become very apparent that my former wife would still be gone whether all my questions were answered or not.

We spend so much time blaming others or coming up with false blame, when we really should be trusting in God for the true answers — or in some cases, no definitive answers. Just as Job questioned God for the calamities that Satan had been allowed to inflict him with - we do not necessarily get the full answers from God.

That is why the quote at the start of this chapter is so relevant. We must trust in the Lord with all our hearts and not rely on our human understandings, even if questions remain. We should truly humble ourselves before the Lord and recognize that He is in control.

Abraham certainly trusted in the Lord, even if he did not see God's promises fulfilled in his lifetime. Abraham could not possibly envision that the Lord would do just as He promised in these verses.

> *"By Myself I have sworn, says the Lord, because you have done this thing, and have not withheld your son, your only son—blessing I will bless you, and multiplying I will multiply your descendants as the stars of the heaven and as the sand which is on the seashore; and your descendants shall possess the gate of their enemies."*

---Genesis 22:16–17

We must take the example from Abraham's life. He trusted in the Lord when human answers weren't as apparent as he would have liked while he lived on this earth. My life changed at the start of my wife's death and change was more profound after my son's death. If God chose to bring me closer to Him, to more fully trust Him as the result of my two loses, - who am I to argue?

I was a member of my church's missionary efforts. Twelve of us went down to Peru in 2008 to help a church that was situated in a remote village where they did not even have electricity. We had to come up with our funding to make the trip. I decided to go, along with my teenage daughter.

Worries over how I was going to pay for this endeavor were an issue, but I soon realized that God, in His Sovereignty, would provide the means for us to make that trip, as He most certainly did.

We spent fifteen days down there. Our eventual destination was the small village of Santa Cruz—a distance of maybe 50 miles from the major city of Tarapoto on the eastern side of the Andes. We journeyed a road that was barely passable by vehicles that we hired to take us to our destination. At one point, we met guards on the road, with AK-47s guarding a particular section and they stopped our small minivan both coming and going. When I thought of it in my flesh, there was a huge potential problem. If these guards did not get the right answers to their questions as to why we wanted to pass by or if they hated Christians, we might have all been shot because violence is a thing that is often overlooked in third-world countries. We were far away from any kind of civilization; drug-running was an issue in the area. As it turned out through our interpreter, we could pass by with a small donation, around sixty cents after the conversion rate. The sovereignty of God had protected us in our encounter, as well as throughout our trip.

Many other things that turned out to be lessons from God remain with me to this day. Certainly, the faith of these people in this village was genuine and not hindered by the fear being spread by the News Media. They had so little in the way of materialistic things that we enjoy in America, yet their true joy in their faith in God is not affected by what they don't have. We ended up building pews for their church, a structure made from mud bricks. We whitewashed those mud bricks on the interior with the materials we either bought to this village or had shipped in. We also built steps to the church because it is situated on a small hill that gets very muddy and slick when it rains. And, because the village is in the area of the rain forest, it rains a lot there. We brought in a gas generator to power our hand tools, which we used to make the pews and the huge wooden cross that we hung in the front of the church. I remember one big, burly man from their village who decided to help us by sanding the rough mahogany boards, that we had bought from a sawmill down there. He took our big belt sander and he was working up quite a sweat moving the heavy sander back and forth across the boards, which would eventually be the seats of these pews. The light in his eyes was precious as one of us showed him how to turn on the sander. This man was so excited that he ended up sanding everything and wore out quite a few of our sanding belts.

Personally, I took along a few Spanish Bibles, along with a Spanish-English parallel Bible—which I picked for free at the secondhand store that I frequented in America. I gave one of the Spanish Bibles to the pastor's wife with instructions for her to distribute it to a child who was particularly needful of the Word. On the day we left, I saw the child she had selected clutching that Bible in her arms as the most precious thing she owned. Next time I go and if God directs me to go, I am going to pack less clothing and fill my suitcases with Spanish Bibles. We do take for granted our availability of the Word here in America.

Very few of us could converse in the particular form of the Spanish language they used, but it was surprising how easily we could adopt hand motions to communicate. Certain phrases like "Jesus loves you" in their form of Spanish--- which I don't exactly remember now, were easily learned. The universal language of love and Jesus Christ has no language barriers.

Overall the trip was filled with many lessons for me, especially the fact that I could trust in the sovereignty of God.

Since that trip, my family in America has adopted a more frugal approach to the things that supposedly make our lives easier. We must distinguish between what is an actual luxury and what is essential and always resist conformity {Romans 12:2}, The basic thing is to be content in what you have and is not what you think you need. The writer of Hebrews certainly makes that point.

> *Let your conduct be without covetousness; be content with such things as you have. For He Himself has said, "I will never leave you nor forsake you."*
>
> **---Hebrews 13:3**

CHAPTER 16

Peace is in casting away our Fears

*There is no fear in love; but **perfect love casts out fear**, because fear involves torment. But he who fears has not been made perfect in love*

---1 John 4:18

I have found that verse to be so true in an application, that the more I practice this perfect love Christ has given me, my fears seem to disappear. I have developed many habits of expressing this love that I try to hold onto.

One example is going to sing Christian Hymns and songs in 3 Nursing Homes each month. After I share my music, I tend to be more peaceful and the fears over the future with my problems seem to go away. Many of the residents in these Nursing Homes are essentially forgotten by their families and one must put themselves into their "shoes" in a sense. You find that you can deal with their problems of dementia and in my example, refresh some of their old memories of songs they have heard as a child. I am learning to look forward to each time I can go to share my music as it does so much for me as I hope it does for them.

I admit that I have not yet been made perfect in love, but then it is a worthwhile goal to always strive for, along with further developing my peace with Christ. The world is watching us Believers and a kind word or a smile to someone will have a much better effect than one of anger or an expression of discontent.

We all have contrary people that we sometimes must deal with. I try to remember the many times God has diffused many situations where I was faced with issues over these encounters and then I put my Trust in Him once again. A short prayer made [even in your mind] can bring back that Trust in Him when you are faced with someone who is very contrary.

While I live in a state now where crime is relatively non-existent, I have spent many years of my life living in bigger cities and have certainly traveled in them. I have had many life-threatening experiences. I was even shot at when the restaurant I was managing was robbed at gunpoint down in Colorado several years ago. After the perpetrator robbed this restaurant, I followed him to the parking lot wanting to at least get his license plate number. He shot at me, but I think it was more that he wanted to scare me. His potential motive certainly worked as I jumped behind a metal trash receptacle. Other incidents that I can relate but the main thing is that people often worry even fear about life needlessly. Of course, our news media will certainly add to those fears if we let them. Christ said it very distinctly here:

> *And do not **fear** those who kill the body but cannot kill the soul. But rather **fear** Him who is able to destroy both soul and body in hell.*

> ---**Matthew 10:28**

Certainly, I am not going to win fans from some gun enthusiasts, but the fears we can adopt by accumulating more weaponry; because of those fears that are being spread like cancer in our society, - that is a huge problem. I have witnessed the huge carnage a gun will do to a person of course and while I have lived around guns for most of my early life. I even won a couple of marksman ribbons years ago and so much of the debate now is senseless. Years ago, my family used them mainly for hunting - not for defense in a society where this huge cancer of fear is being spread at present and it really is this false fear that drives a person to accumulate more high powered weaponry.

I heard the notion from a pastor at one time which is this:

"if you think you need an assault rifle with a hundred shot clip for hunting a deer, maybe you need to pick up another hobby".

One must always check their hearts against these verses in Matthew 24.

> *¹¹ Then many false prophets will rise up and deceive many. ¹²*
> *And because lawlessness will abound, the love of many will*
> *grow cold. ¹³ But he who endures to the end shall be saved.*

---Matthew 24:11-13

It is yet another warning from Christ about these false prophets deceiving many and it is in our reactions to this lawlessness that is abounding is oftentimes where the problems arise. Society has developed a cold love towards those who might think differently, and we think we supposedly must arm ourselves against those imaginary forces of evil in others and of course tends to make our love turn cold. Satan certainly must enjoy the divisions he can cause through many deceptive tactics.

And, a big part of the Nation wanting the Border Wall is born of this cold love condition that is ever so present in our society. Some people are only concerned about abortion but then lose focus on the lives of those Immigrant families and even the children, that is being created at present.

CHAPTER 17

Peace is in Sharing the "Yoke" with Christ

*29 Take My yoke upon you and learn from Me, for I am [a]
gentle and lowly in heart, and you will find rest for your
souls. 30 For My yoke is easy and My burden is light.*

---Matthew 11:29-30

Often when reading Scripture, we must consider the historical context of the verse. A "yoke" is not used much anymore to relate to a form of working or sharing burdens but it did very much in the past.

Basically, when reading and understanding this verse, I like to think of the yokes used by the early settlers in this Country who used a yoke with their oxen to take their covered wagons westward. Or, when they arrived, a yoke with horses or oxen would also be used to pull a plow before we had motorized tractors of course. The basic principle is that a team of oxen or horses had a yoke to share in the load and two yoked together can pull something much better.

The verse applies to doing it all on our own OR accept Christ's help in the burdens of life. Christ simply is offering to share with your burdens in life and accept the yoke He is offering to share here. I simply try to remember a verse here:

I can do all things through Christ who strengthens me.

Philippians 4:13

For those who might be reading this book and have gotten this far, the verse above is yet another Promise from God that has been fulfilled in my life by looking back.

CHAPTER 18

Peace in Living in your God-Given Conscience

This *being* so, I myself always strive to have a **conscience** without offense toward God and men

---Acts 24:16

Something that is little talked about in Christianity is our conscience. We can bruise our conscience and then not go to the Lord with a repentant heart to ask for forgiveness for our sins. Or we can be like this in our total deception.

speaking lies in hypocrisy, having their own **conscience** *seared with a hot iron,*

---I Timothy 4:2

And of course, this verse to consider:

To the pure all things are pure, but to those who are defiled and unbelieving nothing is pure; but even their mind and **conscience** *are defiled.*

---Titus 1:15

You simply cannot find the Peace of God if your conscience is defiled or seared. One obvious way that our conscience can be defiled is with our fleshly opinions and the words we post on social media when we claim these often passed along lies. Do not bear false witness is one of the Commandments but we sometimes overlook it all when we vent our fleshly opinions. James tells us this:

> *If anyone among you thinks he is religious, and does not bridle his **tongue** but deceives his own heart, this one's religion is useless*

> **---James 1:26**

It amazes me that particularly in this political climate around us that there is very little show or concern about the "tongue". People can vent their opinions [that they garnered from their favorite brand of News commentary] and seemingly they act as if they have no concern if they or these "talking heads" have all the facts. "Tongue" can easily be shown to mean our computer keyboards or modern cellphones because it still is a means of "airing our opinions" in a potentially destructive way. But then there is somewhat of permanent record of what we once thought or said on particularly social media—which provides a second chance to repent of our sinfulness.

The effects of living under these deceiving forces are very severe and can cause many non-Believers to question Christianity in general.

> *The purpose of my instruction is that all believers would be filled with love that comes from a pure heart, **a clear conscience**, and genuine faith.*

> **---1 Timothy 1:5 {NLT]**

> "You must not pass along false rumors. You must not cooperate with evil people by lying on the witness stand.

> "You must not follow the crowd in doing wrong. When you are called to testify in a dispute, do not be swayed by the crowd to twist justice.

> **---Exodus 23:1-2 [NKJV]**

This, of course, a Command from the Lord to Moses in the Torah that all the Jewish people should have been familiar with.

One thing that the Pharisees forgot [and certainly the crowd they were leading] was when they demanded Christ's Crucifixion. How very dangerous it is in being part of a crowd and that persuasiveness is in the application.

> So Pilate, wanting to gratify the **crowd**, released Barabbas to them; and he delivered Jesus, after he had scourged *Him,* to be crucified.
>
> ---**Mark 15:15**

I often think "What if I had been a Member of that crowd that day?" What if I had been led to also demand Christ's Crucifixion? That my conscience would have been defiled afterward when I realized I had also demanded the Crucifixion of the Lord.

Instead, we must always go back to these two verses in particular:

> *And this I pray, that your love may abound still more and more in knowledge and all* **discernment***,*
>
> ---**Philippians 1:9**

> [20] *Do not despise prophecies.* [21] *Test all things; hold fast what is good.* [22] *Abstain from every form of evil.*
>
> ---**1 Thessalonians 5:20-22**

CONCLUSION

Depart from evil and do good; Seek peace and pursue it

---Psalms 34:14

We can conclude that having a goal of pursuing the peace of God in one's life is a natural state, even though we are living in this fallen world. An existence we all are searching for, - whether we realize it or not. But then our pride even our own sinfulness can provide a barrier of sorts to existing in that peace. We are simply searching for that existence which Adam and Eve lost through their disobedience [resulting from their pride] which we adopt in many ways. Satan has simply set up a lot of roadblocks that we sometimes have to find our way around with a pure Trust in God in our lives. Satan has many ways in which he can bring that human pride out and that is our problem.

God is His Perfect Solution to our dilemma has sent Christ into the world to help us find our way back to the existence where we have Peace with God, - if we Believe fully in Him.

> *Peace I leave with you, My peace I give to you; not as the world gives do I give to you. Let not your heart be troubled, neither let it be afraid.*

---John 14:27

I believe my life has been one filled with many tests on Faith; and through it has brought a clearer understanding in me of this Peace. Certainly I could have gone through worse situations, but the main thing is I believe God has brought me through the right tests at the right time to get me to the point that I could never deny my faith, thus, I've found my way back to this peace that passes all understanding in any situation that God provides for me, or I strive to find my way back to that peace. It has been a worthwhile endeavor to strive to find my way back to this Peace in any situation through prayer and going back to His Word.

As I look back at the day my son took his life and what I witnessed, it was certainly one in which I could have gone over the edge had not Christ entered my life and stopped me from my running away from Him. It is my prayer that someone may read my book and find the solid Hope and Peace that I have found. We serve a Christ who is the way, the truth, and the life, as He claimed in John 14:6. Through that verse, we can find His peace and overcome any obstacle that comes before us.

> *And He said to me, "**My grace is sufficient for you**, for My strength is made perfect in weakness." Therefore, most gladly I will rather boast in my infirmities, that the power of Christ may rest upon me.*

> **---2 Corinthians 12:9**

This is the promise I remember whenever I face a new obstacle in life. His grace is sufficient for all situations that may come up; that fact coupled with the following verses makes me feel I am complete.

> *For I am persuaded that neither death nor life, nor angels nor principalities nor powers, nor things present nor things to come, nor height nor depth, nor any other created thing, shall be able to separate us from the love of God which is in Christ Jesus our Lord.*

> **---Romans 8:38–39**

On a further note, I want to share a thought from a Sunday School Class I taught a few years ago to 3rd and 4th graders in my Church.

In one of the Lesson Plans, it suggested that I find a picture which showed someone who is very sorrowful, as a part of a complete picture which would indicate great joy; a picture showing a contrast of emotions, if you think about it a bit.

I found a picture of an artist's rendering of Mary Magdalene crying outside the tomb from the account in the Gospel of John. In that rendering, the Risen Christ was standing right behind her in the complete picture. The Lesson Plan suggested that I make a window in the picture only showing [in this case] the weeping Mary and have the children relate to her sorrow, centered on this verse:

> *But Mary stood outside by the tomb weeping, and as she wept*
> *she stooped down and looked into the tomb*

---John 20:11

Mary was filled with grief over the fact that Christ had "gone" from her and she was in great agony.

To make the Passage in John more relevant to us now-- Mary's agony represents the physical separation from Christ that we all are experiencing in our lives. And then, she finally recognizes Him, Who was standing behind her as the Resurrected Christ by this verse...

Jesus said to her, "Mary!"

She turned and said to Him, "Rabboni!" (which is to say, Teacher).

---John 20:16

One can imagine what great Joy she was feeling at the moment when she physically recognized Christ. She ran to the place where the apostles were hiding to tell them in her excitement.

How much more will we be filled with such great Joy and Peace when we, who have lived our earthly life, through Faith eventually come before Him?

This verse from Revelation describes that:

> *And God will wipe away every tear from their eyes; there shall be **no more** death, **no**r sorrow, **no**r crying. There shall be **no more pain**, for the former things have passed away."*

---Revelation 2:14

As we try to look at our lives from God's perspective, all our anguishes and sorrows for a moment ----will be replaced by great Joy, with an Eternal Existence in that total Peace of God, Who we will stand before.

My words here somewhat follow along with the Song <u>I Can Only Imagine</u>, written by Bart Millard of the band Mercy Me in 1999, The song, of course, soon became the #1 bestselling Christian song of all time. We always must try to look at it all from God's Perspective as we suffer our woes in this life. To trust Him more fully and find the Peace of God that can go on the rest of our lives.